BUSINESS EXCELLENCE

Exceeding Your Customers' Expectations Each Time, All the Time

SURESH PATEL

CRC Press
Taylor & Francis Group
Boca Raton London New York

CRC Press is an imprint of the
Taylor & Francis Group, an **informa** business

A PRODUCTIVITY PRESS BOOK

CRC Press
Taylor & Francis Group
6000 Broken Sound Parkway NW, Suite 300
Boca Raton, FL 33487-2742

Library of Congress Cataloging-in-Publication Data

Names: Patel, Suresh (Quality management consultant), author.
Title: Business excellence : exceeding your customers' expectations each time, all the time / Suresh Patel.
Description: 1 Edition. | Boca Raton : CRC Press, [2017] | Includes bibliographical references and index.
Identifiers: LCCN 2016002060 | ISBN 9781498751247
Subjects: LCSH: Organizational effectiveness. | Strategic planning.
Classification: LCC HD58.9 .P378 2016 | DDC 658--dc23
LC record available at https://lccn.loc.gov/2016002060

Visit the Taylor & Francis Web site at
http://www.taylorandfrancis.com

and the CRC Press Web site at
http://www.crcpress.com

I dedicate this book to Mr. K.K. Nair, executive director, Ahmedabad Management Association (AMA), who has encouraged me to write it after observing an excellent feedback from the delegates at the first ever Lean Six Sigma three-day course at the AMA in June, 2011.

I also dedicate this book to my dear wife, Pushpa, who had to bear many disruptions and inconveniences without my help, and without whose full cooperation, this book would not have materialized.

Contents

Foreword

1. If you believe in a product, don't give it up halfway through. Be on it. You will succeed one day and the results will be good.
2. Have patience during difficult times. Don't lose your balance, and try to carry the team with you.
3. If it is a new business, plan for 50% more to standby so that you don't have to close the business or run away.
4. There is a lot of scope in manufacturing. The world's emerging economies can become strong in the long run only through the manufacturing base, and not the service base. A service base is only temporary. This will not create long-term employment.

Suresh met me a month ago and requested that I write a foreword for his sister books: *The Global Quality Management System: Improvement through Systems Thinking*; *Lean Transformation: Cultural Enablers and Enterprise Alignment*; *The Tactical Guide to Six Sigma Implementation*; and *Business Excellence: Exceeding Your Customers' Expectations Each Time, All the Time.*

When I met Suresh, and came to know about his operational excellence experience of more than two decades with multinational corporations like Eaton Corporation and Fiat Global, a bell rang inside me and I made up my mind not only to pen the foreword but also to leverage his Spanish language command to boost the performance of one of my South American Chilean units engaged in manufacturing wear-resistant products and material handling for the mining industry.

I knew Suresh well when I invited him to our Kolkata headquarters, to spend one week at the Tega head office and the main plant at Joka, Kolkata. It was evident from the feedback report I received from my plant management team that these sister books will clear the "cobwebs" and prepare any organization for the journey of continuous quality improvement.

These sister books are unique and comprehensive "how to understand and implement" a Global Quality Management System, Lean System, Six Sigma methodology, and Business Excellence Strategy to achieve world-class business excellence. The author has succinctly summarized the business excellence concept and the body of knowledge of this book by illustrating the business excellence pyramid with the following foundations: Management Systems at the system level, Lean System at the operational level, Six Sigma methodology at the tactical level, and Business Excellence at the strategy level.

The Global Quality Management System: Improvement through Systems Thinking is about the Global Quality Management System (GQMS). It starts by paying homage to leading Quality "gurus." Having illustrated systems thinking as opposed to the command and control system, the author then stresses the fact that command and control system can at worst "influence people to behave in ways which dissatisfy the customer and/or sub-optimize performance."

The main emphasis of any quality management system is on the process. *The Global Quality Management System: Improvement through Systems Thinking* stresses the importance of the process—its identification, definition, improvement, and control using "Turtle" diagram and its extension to "SIPOC" (suppliers, inputs, process, outputs, and customers) diagrams. The processes discussed include, among others, main business processes such as the HR (Human Resource) Process, the Finance Process, the Project Management Process, and, importantly, the "Process of improving the Process."

Every documented GQMS has focus on customer requirements and management system processes, which lead to customer satisfaction. To this end, the author has included advanced processes to comply with ISO 9001, ISO/TS 16949, and AS 9100 standards, and elaborated on management improvement through extensive PDCA (Plan–Do–Check–Act) analysis and the problem-solving methodology involving the famous eight disciplines process ("8D"). The "Check" and "Act" phases are discussed extensively through audit processes and a PCPA process (Process Control Plan Audit) as practiced by most automotive and multinational corporations.

Lean Transformation: Cultural Enablers and Enterprise Alignment is about the Lean System. Section I explains why Lean Implementation usually fails. It goes on to show the approach for Lean Transformation by highlighting the "Cultural Enablers" for the employees (including the management) and how management should align the Lean Transformation process. In Section II, the book explains principles of continuous process. Section III is about the Lean Tools and how they can be deployed for continuous improvement. Section IV is about Lean Performance Measures and how to assess Lean performance. Assessment of the Lean system tools is a very interesting feature of this part and enables an organization to remain focused on the standardization of the Lean System and boost the organization's sustainability efforts.

The author has succinctly portrayed the main principles of the Lean System as follows:

1. Define customer requirement correctly and arrive at customer value so that you are providing what the customer actually wants.
2. Identify the value stream for each product/service family and remove the non-value-added (wasted) steps for which the customer will not pay and that don't create value.
3. Make the value stream flow continuously to shorten throughput and delivery time aggressively.
4. Allow the customer to pull product/service from your value streams as needed (rather than pushing products toward the customer on the basis of forecasts).
5. Never relent until you reach perfection, which is the delivery of pure value instantaneously with zero waste and zero defects.

The Tactical Guide to Six Sigma Implementation is about the unique way in which the so-called difficult concept and practice of Six Sigma methodology are depicted. It includes the collection of tools needed for all five phases: Define, Measure, Analyze, Improve, and Control (DMAIC) and proven best practices to identify which few process and input variables influence the process output measures. To begin with, the author describes the basic concepts of variation, spread of data, and Sigma through basic statistical concepts. Before embarking on the five phases (DMAIC), the author clarifies what is needed for business performance measurement through the concepts of "Balanced Scorecard" and important measuring units for quality performance. Notable measures discussed are DPMO (defects per million opportunities), Rolled Throughput Yield, Cost of Poor Quality (COPQ), Business Failure Costs, Cost–Benefit Analysis, Return on Assets (ROA), and, lastly, a method of evaluating projects and investments known as Net Present Value (NPV) or Discounted Cash Flow (DCF).

The five phases (DMAIC) form the bulk of *The Tactical Guide to Six Sigma Implementation*. The step-by-step approach taken by the author to explain the key concepts and tools required in each one of these phases requires special mention.

Define Phase: Starts with the definition of the VOC or the Voice of the Customer. Here, the QFD (Quality Function Deployment) tool is described in a simple and easy way to translate the customer's voice into the language of the engineer. The QFD is then utilized to define and document a Business Improvement Project Charter based on the customer and competitive intelligence data. The project tracking tools such as Gantt chart, Critical Path Analysis (CPA), and Project Evaluation and Review Technique (PERT) are explained in detail. The Critical to Quality (CTQ) flow-down is introduced to define the customer satisfaction in four areas: Quality, Delivery, Cost, and Safety for internal and external customers.

Measure Phase: The author has identified and discussed 16 different aspects of process characteristics. Having done this, MSA (Measurement System Analysis) is described in great detail to ensure that the integrity of the measured data of important characteristics, the measuring equipment, and the human aspect of the measurement system are maintained within allowed R&R (Repeatability and Reproducibility) acceptance criteria.

Analyze Phase: Here, the root cause analysis methods for the problems encountered are discussed. The main techniques described include regression and correlation, ANOVA, FMEA, Gap Analysis, Waste Analysis, and Kaizen.

Improve Phase: The process improvement methods discussed in this phase are prioritization through C & E Matrix (Cause-and-Effect Matrix), Kaizen using Lean Tools and Six Sigma, PDCA, and Theory of Constraints.

Control Phase: Key concepts and tools illustrated in the control phase are SPC (Statistical Process Control), TPM and OEE (Total Productive Maintenance and Overall Equipment Effectiveness), MSA, Control Plan, and Visual Factory. In order to sustain the improvements, the tools referred to are as follows: Lessons Learned, Training Plan, SOPs (Standard Operating Procedures), Work Instruction, and ongoing performance assessment.

The **DFSS (Design for Six Sigma)** methodology is a very useful and logical extension of the Six Sigma phases. The tools discussed in DFSS include DMADV (Define, Measure, Analyze, Design, and Verify) and DMADOV (Design, Measure, Analyze, Design, Optimize, and Verify). Design for X (DFX) includes reliability analysis and design of tolerance limits. Special design tools described are Porter's five forces analysis and TRIZ (Russian for "Theory of Inventive Problem Solving").

Any Six Sigma book cannot be called complete without a case study. To this end, the author has chosen an improvement project to improve the batting in the Cricket Game using Lean Six Sigma approach.

Business Excellence: Exceeding Your Customers' Expectations Each Time, All the Time is about Business Excellence Strategy. There are many models of Business Excellence practiced by many countries of the world. At best, these models lay down Business Excellence Assessment criteria, but the author has felt that the main requirement of the organizations intending to embark on business strategy is a special body of knowledge with which the Business Excellence strategy can be implemented successfully. The inclusion of strategies for Leadership, Strategic Planning, Customer Excellence, Operational Excellence, and Functional Excellence for HR and IT will prove to be very useful for the initiated management. Assessment of Business Excellence strategy through the use of the Balanced Scorecard, Employee Survey, Achieving Performance Excellence, and Cost Out is a very effective chapter for the Business Excellence Strategy.

Finally, as you will put these sister books of knowledge into practice, you will find out the shifting roles of leaders and managers in your organization. It is not enough for the leaders to just keep on doing what they have always done. It is not enough for them to merely support the work of others. Rather, leaders must lead the cultural transformation and change the mind-sets of their associates by building on the principles behind all these excellent tools.

The author's account of these difficult and vast subjects is very praiseworthy and a proof of his vast industrial experience of more than four decades working with MNCs in Asia, Europe, and the Americas. This is an inspirational work that is easy to be learned and applied by the lay reader. I highly recommend this book to all students, teachers, executives, and organizations who want to learn and implement GQMS Lean Six Sigma systems and Business Excellence strategies.

Madan Mohanka
CMD and Founder
TEGA Industries Limited
Kolkata

Preface

Quality and Business Excellence sister books create and deploy the preventive quality culture within an organization. These sister books enhance customer value and satisfaction by fully integrating the customer's voice into design, manufacturing, supply chain, and field processes.

Almost all business organizations are engaged in providing services or products to their customers, but when it comes to providing service to customers and presenting them an experience that will make them come back time and time again, only a small minority of organizations stand out from the crowd who apply the energy, commitment, and innovative thinking to get it right. There is an enormous difference between those who are truly focused on customers and those who simply pay lip service.

These sister books have been written primarily for business entrepreneurs, business managers, engineering managers, and technocrats who wish to grasp Global Quality, Lean, Six Sigma, and Business Excellence concepts, methodologies, and tools to improve and to promote their companies to world-class standard for profitability and sustainability.

These sister books can be used as a basic textbook for a Green Belt, Black Belt, BBA, and MBA course in Global Quality, Lean Six Sigma, and Business Excellence.

The word *quality* has been applied in many enterprises, mostly by quality professionals and consultants. Lately, the word *quality* is replaced by *continuous improvement*. These two words have become *continual improvement* in ISO 9000 standards and have now finally become *continuous quality improvement*. The subsequent proliferation of terms tends to confuse managers in the marketplace. ISO9001, ISO/TS16949, AS 9100, JIT (Just in Time), MBNQA (Malcolm Baldrige National Quality Award), Six Sigma, Kaizen, Kanban, 5S, Lean, TPM (Total Productive Maintenance), TQM (Total Quality Management), and so on, are only a few of the initiatives confronting organizational leaders. No wonder managers are confused. Too many consultants are trying to sell the next "fad" or a "savior" to gain an advantage in the marketplace.

These sister books clear the cobwebs. It prepares the initiated person/ organization for the journey of continuous improvement. The guiding principle is

> An organization must constantly measure the effectiveness of its processes and strive to meet more difficult objectives to satisfy customers.

Taiichi Ohno
Toyota Production System

Acknowledgments

Acknowledging the help and guidance in writing these sister books is to me like churning the oceans of the world and putting all the blessings in a tea cup. I find it very daunting because during my more than 50 years of industry experience, I have been guided and helped by many persons, companies, and institutions with whose associations, I have learned, practiced, and taught these subjects and achieved modest to excellent results.

After I decided to return to Ahmedabad from Texas, Prof. R.D. Patel, finance professor at IIM Ahmedabad, asked me to address their SME program as a guest speaker to talk about Lean Six Sigma. The feedback from the attendees was good and he (Prof. Patel) took me to AMA (Ahmedabad Management Association) to meet with its executive director, K.K. Nair, who asked me to conduct a first-ever five-day AMA Lean Six Sigma seminar attended by industry representatives from Rajkot, Vadodara, Surat, and Ahmedabad. This led to another seminar at AMA and an invitation by the HR Head of ISRO (equivalent to Indian NASA) J. Ravisankar to address ISRO technicians and engineers on the subject of zero defects delivery of space systems, which was well received.

All of the above led K.K. Nair to ask me to write a book on Lean Six Sigma for Indian engineers. My learning and experience as an operations excellence and engineering manager at Eaton Corporation (Eden Prairie, Minnesota) and Fiat Global (Burr Ridge Operations, Chicago, Illinois) made me to take a holistic view and include Global Quality Management System at the bottom rung and Business Excellence at the top level. So I wound up writing four books.

I thank the following individuals for their contributions to my knowledge and all the help and guidance they offered to me in my career, which resulted in creating these books: C.S. Patel, former CEO of Anand Group of leading automobile companies manufacturing automotive components; the late D.N. Sarkar, CMD of Gestetner Limited; Samir Kagalwala, consultant for the design and manufacture of power magnetics; Stefan Lorincz, renowned electronics engineer and source developer for key electronic components worldwide at Phillips, Holland; Levy Katzir, former Motorola VP, who, in 1994, put me in charge of quality and reliability of the newly developed electronic ballasts; G.P. Reddy, former director of quality at

Universal Lighting Technologies; Inder Khatter, international QMS lead auditor for DNV, Houston, Texas; Dev Raheja, international consultant and co-author of *Assurance Technologies Principles and Practices*; Frank Kobyluch, global general manager at Klein Tools and former plant manager at Eaton Corporation; and Don Johnson, director of quality at Fiat Global–Case New Holland Division.

My special thanks and gratitude to my colleagues and team members at the following companies where I worked, learned, developed, and implemented many of the tools and techniques contained in these books: Gestetner Limited (now Ricoh India); Energy Savings Inc., Schaumburg, Illinois; United Lighting Technologies, Nashville, Tennessee; Eaton Hydraulics, Eden Prairie, Minnesota; and Fiat Global—Case New Holland, Burr Ridge, Chicago, Illinois.

My abilities as an operations excellence manager in charge of providing quality products for CFL ballasts, hydraulic valves, hydraulic pumps, hydraulic hoses, and fittings were honed, tested, and appreciated by customers such as GE CFL Lamps, Osram—Sylvania, John Deere, Case New Holland, and Oshkosh Corporation, manufacturer of severe heavy-duty all-wheel drive defense trucks, Caterpillar, GM trucks, Ford trucks, Volvo trucks, Zamboni Ice resurfacer (for Winter Olympic Games), and so on.

I will remain grateful to the following suppliers who collaborated with me and my team in developing components and major assembly units requiring extremely high precision and pre-/posttreatments: Parker Hannifin supplied high-quality hydraulic seals and O-rings; Bosch, supplier of specialty hydraulic valves; Carraro Pune, supplier of a complete four-speed transmission unit for agricultural tractors; TGL-Carraro Pune, which developed precision gears and shafts for transmission; Carraro, Qingdao China, with whom we developed an entire rear axle assembly for backhoe loaders; Graziano Transmissioni, Noida, India, where we developed a continuously variable transmission unit for a tractor for the first time for the U.S. market; GNA Group Punjab, which supplied us forged and precision machined components for the tractor transmission assemblies; Craftsman Automation Limited, Coimbatore, which machined our large castings for transmission body and covers using heavy CNC machines and digital CMMs.

I have remained in touch with developing technology and professional knowledge through the American Society for Quality, whose membership I have since 1993.

Illustrations and design of charts and figures in these books are done by Sanjay Trivedi and Minal Mehta.

Making It Big in Manufacturing Product and Providing Service

It is a general belief that successful people in every field are blessed with talent or are just lucky. But the fact is successful people work hard, work long, and work smart.

Marissa Ann Mayer, the current president and CEO of Yahoo, used to work 130 hours per week while working at Google. India-born Indra Krishnamurthy Nooyi, chairman and chief executive officer of PepsiCo, worked midnight to 5 a.m. as a receptionist to earn money so that she could complete her master's degree at Yale University. In 1958, Qimat Rai Gupta left his education midway and founded Electric Trading Operations in the electric wholesale market of Old Delhi, India. With an investment of Rs.10000 ($150), he started Havells Industries. Today, Havells is a billion-dollar company. In his own words: "overnight success means 25 years of hard work, devotion and dedication."

The founder and CEO of the Kolkata, India–based Tega Industries, Madan Mohanka's story is unique. When he went into business, he had the right combination—hailing from a business family, having an engineering degree, getting an MBA from IIM Ahmedabad, and having a foreign collaborator as a joint partner. Yet, this combination failed miserably. He was witnessing the imminent closure of his company in 1979, but like the epic hero Odysseus, he never lost focus for a moment. He kept at it. Some three decades later, it is Madan's die-hard optimism that saw Tega Industries become the second largest player in the world in rubber mill lining products for the mining industry.

In her book *Stay Hungry, Stay Foolish*, Rashmi Bansal (IIMA Graduate) depicted Madan Mohanka's hard-won story very aptly. She said Madan faced all hurdles and challenges starting from scratch, but then Madan had what you call an "obsession." Over the last three decades, Madan built a strong foundation combining three technologies, namely, Mechanical Engineering, Rubber (Polymer) Technology, and Mineral Processing and Grinding. Over the last five to six years, Tega accepted challenges, grabbed overseas marketing opportunities, and maintained consistent growth keeping an eye on the margins.

Tega's presence in 19 international locations has enabled it to increase a turnover of $4 million in 2009 to $120 million in 2014.

According to Mehul Mohanka, the U.S.-trained MBA son, the stage is now set for organic and inorganic growth: organically building up larger capabilities and inorganically looking for acquisitions for successful integration with Tega's culture, values, and philosophy.

1

Introduction

This book is about a Business Excellence (BE) strategy that has total customer satisfaction in its foundation. When it comes to satisfying the customer and RETAINING the customer, there is no better statement than what Mahatma Gandhi said:

> A customer is the most important visitor on our premises. He is not dependent on us. We are dependent on him. He is not an interruption in our work. He is the purpose of it. He is not an outsider in our business. He is part of it. We are not doing him a favour by serving him. He is doing us a favour by giving us an opportunity to do so.
>
> **Mahatma Gandhi**

Thus, when it comes to serving customers, and offering them an experience that will make them come back to the products and services offered by you time and time again, a small minority of organizations stand out from the crowd for the energy, commitment, and innovative thinking they apply to do it right. There is a world of difference between those who are truly driven by customer focus and those who simply pay lip service to the ideal, while following a separate agenda. Who are these focused companies? The marketplace offers some clues about which companies are serving their customers best; after all, if you're making profitable sales to millions of customers, you must be doing something right. But that is only part of the story. An organization wanting to sustain and continually improve its competitive performance over many years needs to have a strategy—a BE strategy.

WHAT IS BUSINESS EXCELLENCE?

BE is a powerful integration of proven strategy elements, tools, and processes that will give your company a significant advantage when they are deployed as prescribed across the organization. It is a holistic view that reduces opportunities for suboptimization–optimization ("a situation where a process, procedure, or system yields less than the best possible outcome"—*Business Dictionary*).

A BE initiative could start by studying BE models adopted by many countries. The most common model is the Baldrige Criteria for Performance Excellence. The Baldrige National Quality Program and the associated award were established and enacted in the United States. The law is named as the Malcolm Baldrige National Quality Improvement Act of 1987. The program and award were named for Malcolm Baldrige, who served as U.S. Secretary of Commerce during the Reagan administration, from 1981 until 1987. In 2010, the program's name was changed to the Baldrige Performance Excellence Program to reflect the evolution of the field of quality from a focus on product, service, and customer quality to a broader, strategic focus on overall organizational quality—called Business Performance Excellence.

Every organization understands that achieving performance excellence is imperative in order for it to succeed in today's business world. To achieve this level of excellence, organizations need to operate at many different levels and with many different perspectives. BE models like the Baldrige model create the framework for organizations to think strategically.

As Figure 1.1 illustrates, the Baldrige model focuses on BE. To attain excellence, organizations use a variety of improvement methodologies, such as those shown here. The Baldrige model does not replace these methodologies, but instead integrates these tools and methods to help companies achieve excellence.

Figure 1.1 shows how the excellence pyramid relates to Quality Management System, Lean, and Six Sigma. The Baldrige Criteria, Lean, and Six Sigma are complementary, and not mutually exclusive. Many organizations use Baldrige in preference to other BE models to develop an overall performance map to identify areas that need improvement, and then they use Six Sigma, Lean, or both tools to design operations or improve processes within the organization.

The criteria elements of some of the BE models are shown in Table 1.1.

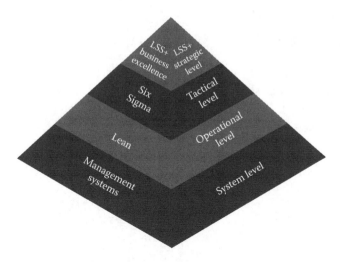

FIGURE 1.1
Excellence pyramid.

TABLE 1.1

The Criteria Elements of Some of the BE Models

Criteria No.	Baldrige Model Called MBNQA (Malcolm Baldrige National Quality Award)	Japan Quality Award	European and India Model Called the EFQM (Formerly Known as the European Foundation for Quality Management) Model
1	Leadership	Leadership	Leadership
2	Strategic planning	Strategic planning	Strategy
3	Customer focus	Customer focus	People, partnerships
4	Measurement, analysis, and knowledge management	Information management	Resources
5	Workforce focus	Individual and organizational; ability to improve	People
6	Operations focus	Value creation process	Process, products, and services
7	Results	Activity results	Results

Note: India has four national quality/BE awards: (1) CII-EXIM Bank Award for Business Excellence (EFQM Excellence Model), (2) Rajiv Gandhi National Quality Award (Rajiv Gandhi National Quality Award criteria), (3) IMC Ramkrishna Bajaj National Quality Award (IMC Ramkrishna Bajaj National Quality Award criteria), and (4) Golden Peacock National Quality Award (Golden Peacock National Quality Award criteria).

BUSINESS EXCELLENCE FRAMEWORK

The Baldrige model creates the framework for BE for organizations to think strategically as shown in Figure 1.2.

The framework connecting and integrating the seven categories has three basic elements.

1. Strategy and Action Plans

Strategy and Action Plans (roof of the figure) yield the set of customer- and market-focused performance requirements, derived from short- and long-term strategic planning, that must be met and exceeded for the organization's strategy to succeed. Strategy and Action Plans guide overall resource decisions and drive the alignment of measures for the organization's work units to ensure customer satisfaction and market success. Preparing an organizational profile detailing the strategy and action plans is a key requirement described later in the chapter.

2. System

The System is composed of the six BE categories in the center of the figure that define the organization, its operations, and its results.

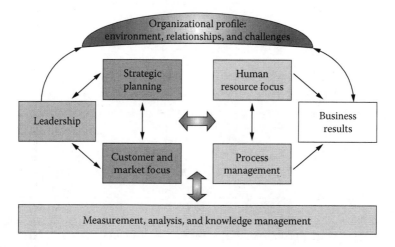

FIGURE 1.2

Baldrige Business Excellence Framework. (Used with permission of the Baldrige Performance Excellence Program. 2015. 2015–2016 Framework for Performance Excellence.)

BUSINESS EXCELLENCE CATEGORIES

Leadership (Category 1), Strategic Planning (Category 2), and Customer and Market Focus (Category 3) represent the leadership triad. These categories are placed together to emphasize the importance of a leadership focus on strategy and customers. Senior leaders must set organizational direction and seek future opportunities for the organization. If the leadership is not focused on customers, the organization as a whole will lack that focus.

Human Resource Focus (Category 5), Process Management (Category 6), and Business Results (Category 7) represent the results triad. An organization's employees and its key processes accomplish the work of the organization that yields its business results.

Category 4: Measurement, Analysis, and Knowledge Management has two main sections:

4.1 Measurement and Analysis, and Review of Organizational Performance
4.2 Information and Knowledge Management

All actions point toward Business Results. The results encompass customer, finance, and operational performance results, including human resource results and public responsibility.

The horizontal arrow in the center of the framework links the leadership triad to the results triad, a linkage critical to organizational success. Furthermore, the arrow indicates the central relationship between Leadership (Category 1) and Business Results (Category 7). Leadership must keep its eyes on Business Results and must learn from them to drive improvement.

3. Information and Analysis

Information and Analysis (Category 4) is critical to the effective management of the organization and to a fact-based system for improving company performance and competitiveness. Information and Analysis serve as a foundation for the performance management system.

As the excellence pyramid illustrates to attain BE, organizations use a variety of improvement methodologies, such as those shown in the pyramid and so far covered in *The Global Quality Management System: Improvement through Systems Thinking, Lean Transformation: Cultural Enablers and Enterprise Alignment, and the Tactical Guide to Six Sigma Implementation.*

The BE model does not replace these methodologies, but instead integrates these tools and methods to help companies achieve excellence.

ROADBLOCKS TO BE TRANSFORMATION

Most organizations want quick fixes and immediate results. If they do not get the immediate reward they seek, they may abandon the program and the team or go in search of the next best thing. This need for immediate results has caused the total abandoning, or limited success, of many improvement programs such as the BE strategy.

Generally, leaders do not understand what it takes to build BE skills and shift mind-sets and behaviors. To think that anyone can come out of a four- to five-day training and have any kind of proficiency is just a mockery. Of course, once they have obtained a label as a BE expert, they are placed in impossible situations and given responsibility to make changes that they are not capable of making. It is possible to gain awareness and understanding of the why behind things—and possibly even the what—in short training, but not the how.

Leaders believe that they can delegate BE, and there is nothing they have to do. The group where the most development needs to be done is leadership. The largest paradigm shift is needed there.

Generally, leaders have the following beliefs:

1. Belief that "the only way to significantly reduce costs is to have layoffs because 80% of the cost structure is labor."
2. Financially oriented people often think that BE is all about cost reductions versus building a flexible and adaptive organization for the future.

As soon as anyone says, "I will use any process improvement method as long as it works," they have limited BE to a process improvement method. BE is about a holistic Business System (BS) and gets to the very purpose of the organization. It includes both the technical and social—it applies to all.

Successful transformation to a BE culture is full of hardships. It requires an enterprise-wide approach that engages the entire organization and challenges its norms and existing practices. It requires knowledge of new tools and methodologies and a level of internal discipline beyond that in which most organizations operate. The BE journey is where the performance indicators continually go up and up. The journey itself is not only exciting but also very rewarding.

Why does the BE strategy work in some organizations and not in others? In short, the difference between success and failure is in cultural acceptance and the ability of an organization to accept change, not just change to the BE strategy, but change in general.

Understanding the mind-set of business is crucial to the success of implementing the BE strategy.

Let us first understand the BS. As we discussed earlier in *Lean Transformation: Cultural Enablers and Enterprise Alignment,* a system is "a group of interacting, interrelated, or interdependent elements forming a complex whole." No system element can function on its own. It has to rely on other elements and has to maintain its relationship with other elements.

The human body is a system where the hands, feet, stomach, heart, and so on are the elements that enable the body to function as a whole. No element can function on its own. Dr. Ackoff once joked; "try cutting off your hand and put it on the table—it won't work!"

Now, let us apply the system concept to business, and as stated in the beginning, how does this translate into implementing BE strategy for a business?

CORE BUSINESS FUNCTIONS

Let us consider a business having the following core functions:

- Sales
- Marketing
- Engineering
- Production
- Customer Service

Figure 1.3 shows the core business functions.

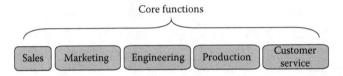

FIGURE 1.3
Core functions.

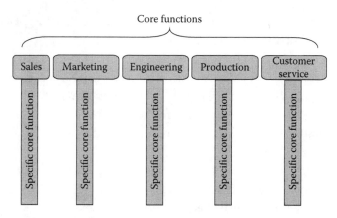

FIGURE 1.4
Core function processes.

CORE FUNCTIONS HAVE THEIR OWN PROCESSES

Each one of these core functions has its own set of defined processes, and it uses its processes to accomplish its goals (Figure 1.4).

CORE BUSINESS SUPPORT FUNCTIONS

Now, apart from the main core functions, business is also supported by support functions such as the following:

- Human Resources
- Finance
- Information Technology (IT)
- Warehousing

Called support functions (Figure 1.5).

At this point, the analysis of the BS looks vertical. Individuals inside a particular functional area have full view of their own process but have difficulty seeing outside of these "silos." They intersect with another functional area only when they need to use a common resource. For example, an intersection between sales and production functional areas occurs when a tracking system managed by the IT support function is used by the production function to deliver a product to a customer. In short, each

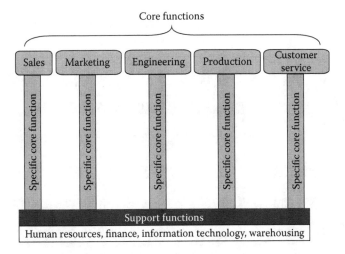

FIGURE 1.5
Support functions for core functions.

individual part of the BS is trying to work on its own. Another example of this "silo" mentality can be commonly seen with engineering when engineering changes are carried out without changing production processes.

This limited perspective is why it is crucial to understand the business processes that cut across these functional process areas.

BUSINESS PROCESS VIEW

A business process is a collection of related activities that produce a product or service of value to the organization, its stakeholders, or its customers.

Let us look at the following examples of main business processes:

- Quote-to-cash
- Procure-to-pay
- New product/service development
- Order fulfillment

Becoming familiar with cross-functional business processes described in Figure 1.6 greatly increases the understanding of the interrelationships between the core functions and clarifies how a quality project in one area of the company will affect other areas (Figure 1.6). This interaction and interdependence among core functions are the key to removing

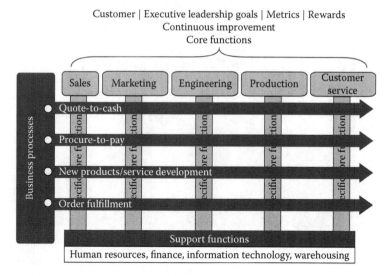

FIGURE 1.6
Typical business processes pass through all core functions.

the roadblocks in implementing a BE strategy. However, we must consider another aspect of the business process: **Its Purpose**.

MANAGING THE PURPOSE

No business process can be effective unless the purpose is properly communicated to all stakeholders. Figure 1.7 shows the main purpose of the organization. Executive leadership should drive management on the business purpose and impress upon all members of the organization the importance of understanding and fulfilling that purpose. The purpose is to improve continuously through set goals, metrics, and rewards (Figure 1.7). In addition, the leadership must govern, manage, adjust, and reset the purpose based on customer needs and other factors.

PROCESS IMPACT ON THE ORGANIZATION

A BE strategy recognizes that there are many input, output, and feedback sources for an organization. Each output may have its own process

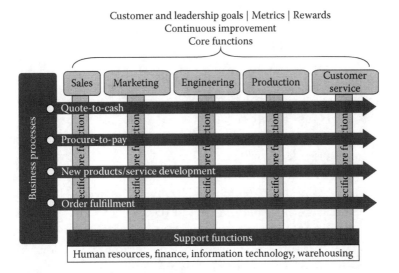

FIGURE 1.7
The purpose of an organization is to meet goals.

dependent on the input from other processes. All inputs and outputs of a particular process should be measurable so that quality can be controlled (Figure 1.8).

Suppliers, Inputs, Process, Outputs, and Customers (SIPOC) is a tool that can be used to help identify these processes in an organization. Here, it is important to know that improvements in one area may create errors in another.

In the *Global Quality Management* book, we have seen that there are many input, output, and feedback processes for an organization. All inputs and outputs of a particular process should be measurable so that quality can be controlled (Figure 1.8).

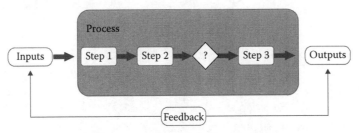

Conduct measurements at both points to gauge
the efficiency and effectiveness of the process.

FIGURE 1.8
Process inputs and outputs with feedback and measurement points.

To truly grasp the system, however, we must avoid the following traps:

- Not approaching BS as a system—and deploying the elements and tools separately.
- Approaching BE assessments as ways to demonstrate compliance rather than as ways to demonstrate meaningful improvement in processes and results within your businesses and functions.
- Seeing BS elements as obligations in addition to your jobs instead of better ways to do your jobs.
- Here are important thoughts:
  - If we continue to fail to capitalize on the synergies between and among the elements and tools of BS...
  - If we continue to approach assessments as demonstrations of compliance and fail to insist that our improvement efforts lead to meaningful improvement in performance...
  - If we continue to see BS deployment as an obligation that is tacked on to our real jobs ... we will continue to be part of a company that can taste greatness, but just can't quite pull off greatness.
- We can't expect to take apart a system and have it achieve its greatest potential. If we focus our attention on some components while ignoring or just going through the motions with others, we get a system that is out of balance. We get a system that can't achieve its true potential.

Having warned ourselves against the possible pitfalls, let us now chart out a BS framework on the basis of the main criteria of the BE models.

BS FRAMEWORK

The functions of the BE are as follows:

- Leadership (Foundation)
- Strategic Planning
- Growth
- Operational Excellence
- Functional Excellence
- Assessment
- Training and Learning

Table 1.2 shows the BS framework.

TABLE 1.2

BS Framework

Leadership	T	Strategic Planning	T	Customer Excellence	T	Operational and Process Excellence	T	Functional Excellence	T	Assessment
Vision		Strategic plan		Value-based pricing and customer value management		Global quality system (*The Global Quality Management System: Improvement through Systems Thinking*)		HR systems		Performance management
Values		Profit plan		Corporate growth through customer and market knowledge		Lean for operational excellence (*Lean Transformation: Cultural Enablers and Enterprise Alignment*)		IT		Balanced scorecard
Goals		OCA (organizational capability assessment)		Corporate growth through customer relationships and satisfaction		Six Sigma tactical methodology (*The Tactical Guide to Six Sigma Implementation*)		Finance, legal, company affairs are not included in this book		Business results
Mission						Operational excellence				Business excellence assessment
Ethics						Acquisition integration				
Corporate policies in each functional area						Capital optimization				
Philosophy										
Learning										

Note: T, training and learning for each functional aspect should be planned through courses, self-study, councils, on-the-job training, and Kaizen.

PLAN FOR CHANGE, INTRODUCTION OF THE BE STRATEGY IN THE ORGANIZATION

a. Plan for Change

Here, we need to consider two parallel complementary organizations. One is the existing organization and the second is an internal BE promotional organization called an organization for change. It may be headed by an Operational Excellence (OpEx) manager or an equivalent person fully supported by necessary resources and the top management. He or she will be assisted by a Kaizen committee charged with learning, training, educating, and initiating the implementation of each of the functional aspects described in Table 1.2 for the BS framework.

The Kaizen committee (team) formation and its work are described in great detail in *Lean Transformation: Cultural Enablers and Enterprise Alignment*, a sister to this book.

The important tasks of the committee are as follows:

1. The committee will be a homogeneous group committed to change. It will consist of line managers who can use examples from their fields of work and expertise.
2. A gap analysis tool is used to identify a performance difference between a current state and a desired or future state. Buy the criteria published by the BE model, for example, the 2015–2016 criteria of the Malcolm Baldrige National Quality Award (MBNQA) model. Find the gaps in each functional aspect by comparing the existing function with the desired function as laid down in the BE model. The desired or future state may be set by recognizing the potential performance determined through such activities as benchmarking or through organizational strategic planning. For example, the annual goal may turn into an intermediate goal next year and an intermediate goal may turn into a noble or ultimate goal the year after the next.
3. The committee will unite learning with implementation by following the learn, apply, and learn (LAL) process.
4. The main steps of the LAL process are as follows:
   - Approach
   - Deployment
   - Learning
   - Integration

Approach

- Define and identify the methods used to accomplish the process.
- Methods are appropriated to the BE criteria requirements and are effective.
- Describe the process of a function through documentation or by using a SIPOC diagram (*The Global Quality Management System: Improvement through Systems Thinking*) to address the process requirements.
- The approach includes the appropriateness of the methods to the process requirements and the effectiveness of their use.
- Approach includes study of all multiple requirements of the process and it is fully responsive to these requirements.
- This approach will be repeatable and systematic and will be based on reliable data.
- Through this approach, it becomes easy to train all levels of employees who use this process.

Deployment

- Utilization of Kaizen teams that drive action plans.
- Heavy reliance on the BS, especially in the area of Lean, Six Sigma, and Global Quality System.
- The approach is applied consistently, meaning it is reviewed and improved as necessary based on changed customer requirements, customer complaints, or employee suggestions. The modified procedure (new revision) is communicated to all concerned using an "I have read it and understood it" procedure.
- This approach is used by all work units through an intranet-based quality system documentation and engineering documentation.

Learning

- The approach is redefined through regular cycles of improvement twice per year. The improvements come through corrective actions on the basis of customer complaints, employee inputs for improvement, and Lean Kaizen efforts.
- Breakthrough change to the approach is encouraged through LEAN Kaizen and innovation in product design to serve customers' anticipated needs, for example, introducing alternative material in a

product, one-piece design combining two separate parts, reducing transaction cost through automation.

- All these changes are documented and communicated to all concerned through changed Value Stream Maps, Process Failure Mode Effects Analyses, work instructions, and tooling changes as required.
- The refined processes and innovations (as applicable) are shared with other organization partners.

Integration

- This process approach is aligned with other organizational requirements like strategic planning by defining process metrics and monitoring their effectiveness and efficiency.
- The approach is aligned with the stakeholder's needs.
- Forms the backbone of the plan–do–check–act (PDCA) for overall plant leadership system.
- Integrates with Global Quality Management System (GQMS) and Measurement/Analysis systems as the execution arm "to drive" the organization to the next year's goals.
- Synchronizes with reward and recognition systems to drive passionate work culture.
- Heavily integrated into goal setting for a visual and organized approach to the HR Performance Management System.

The last two important activities of this committee are as follows:

1. Promotion: Publish activities of training and education through brochures and fliers as part of the BE implementation project.
2. Such success stories lead to a snowball effect. Hence, combine celebration and fun during the presentation of the success stories.

b. Introduction of the BE Strategy in the Organization

Organizational Profile

- A good starting point will be to prepare and publish an organization chart with the names and position descriptions of the current holders. The next important task will be to prepare an organizational profile set out in the BE model criteria.

- It sets the context for the way the organization operates.
- It summarizes the organization's environment, key working relationships, and strategic challenges.
- It provides the basis for evaluation of the organization.

The profile includes the following:

- Organizational environment
- Organizational relationships
- Competitive environment
- Strategic challenges
- Performance improvement system

Here is an example of a typical organizational profile of an imaginary organization called "Speedy Electronics Limited" (Speedy in short form).

Speedy is a manufacturer of printed electronic circuit boards. 2013 sales of $100-million positions it as the second largest Small and Medium Enterprises (SME) operation within the state of Gujarat, India. Its chairman and managing director, Mr. Racer, started the company as a small-scale supplier to the Indian Space Research Organization in Ahmedabad and went public in 2007. Double-sided circuit boards with surface-mount components were started in 2008, resulting in global scope position.

Channels to market include direct (75%) and distribution (25%). Larger original equipment manufacturers (OEMs) are typically sold direct with distributors handling midsized and small-sized OEMs.

Distributors also serve the aftermarket "user" segment on a retail basis and in some cases offer catalog and Internet sales.

Speedy has a diverse workforce hailing from various states in India with various religious beliefs and practices. The common purpose, vision, mission, values, and global processes act as uniting common threads across the organization. Employee development opportunities, including functional training, are offered within the company.

The tuition reimbursement program funds higher education for employees through accredited technical institutes.

Annual employee surveys measure employee engagement and satisfaction. Survey results help the management select areas of improvement across the organization to enhance the work environment and drive retention.

CORE COMPETENCIES

Speedy core competencies are as follows:

1. Innovative product design using 3D Auto Cad, CNC high-speed drilling, and fully automatic mounting machine for surface-mounted components (SMCs) with inbuilt component quality checking feature
2. Multilayer printed circuit boards for mobile phones

   Speedy takes compliance with governmental and corporate requirements very seriously. It actively pursues certifications per ISO-9001: 2016 and ISO/TS16949:2002. Its manufacturing plant is ISO 14001 certified. SCM, Human Resources, IT, and Finance are organized in a traditional reporting structure (organization chart not given here).

STRATEGIC CHALLENGES

Key strategic issues include the following:

- Within India—redistribute the product mix
- Africa and Middle East—speed up the growth
- Global—differentiated new product development

Process improvement is increasingly becoming a part of the Speedy culture. Primary process improvement tools include Business Process Improvement and Lean Six Sigma. Regular internal assessments help Speedy stay on the path of continuous improvement.

Profile example is complete.

IMPORTANCE OF PREPARING AN ORGANIZATIONAL PROFILE

The purpose of such profile is to determine Key Business Factors (KBFs) for an organization

- KBFs describe significant facts or aspects about the organization
  - A quick snapshot of the organization
  - The operating environment

- Significant working relationships
- Key challenges
- Help focus the criteria in terms of its relevance to the organization

KEY BUSINESS FACTORS

KBFs for Speedy may be extracted from the profile as shown in Table 1.3.

TABLE 1.3

KBF Examples

KBFs for "Speedy"	Cat. 1	Cat. 2	Cat. 3	Cat. 4	Cat. 5	Cat. 6
Proprietary products and services			1			1
Sold to OEMs and end users			1			
In-house R&D, product development process			1			1
Four core processes centered on people, planning, and continuous improvement	1	1				
Employee retention and recruiting	1	1			1	
MRO aftermarket through two distributor agreements to support its customers worldwide			1			
Knowledge management				1	1	
World leader—benchmarking	1	1		1		
Compensation, benefits—is it diving toward improved retention?	1				1	
Empowerment is important … how?	1				1	
Safety—processes and training					1	1
Wide range of products, how to focus?		1	1			
Lean Mfg. and Six Sigma for performance improvements	1			1		1
40% Market share for simple cell phone PCBs		1	1			
Suppliers—small number but important; raw materials; international growth possibilities?		1				1
Regulatory compliance, FAA, environmental, defense regulations, foreign agency	1					
Employee performance review process and goal alignment and employee retention	1			1	1	
Customer requirements: on-site eng. support, rapid prototyping, JIT, reliability			1			1
Competitors are small companies		1	1	1		
	8	7	8	5	6	6

Each factor is related to more than one criterion of the BE categories. This way, when a criterion of the BE model is studied by the Kaizen team, this kind of a snapshot summary keeps the team focused on the particular business factor, and through SWOT analysis and goal-based gap analysis, it steers the team toward achieving excellence.

2

Leadership

The Leadership function examines how the organization's senior leaders guide and sustain the organization. Figure 2.1 shows how the leaders plan, do, check, and act to propel the organization to achieve planned goals. Also examined are the organization's governance and how an organization addresses its ethical, legal, and community responsibilities.

LEADERSHIP SYSTEM

Leadership system is explained through the famous Plan, Do, Check, and Act (PDCA) cycle of continuous improvement.

Plan

This stage has three main steps.

1. Establish direction
   - Foundation including goals and philosophy
   - Organizational capability analysis
   - Strategic plan
2. Set expectations and goals
   - Goal deployment
   - Profit plan
   - Achieving performance excellence (APEX) objectives
3. Organize, plan, prioritize, align resources
   - Go to market
   - District operating plans

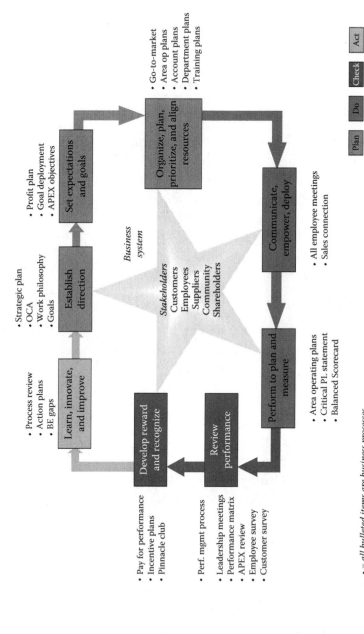

FIGURE 2.1
Leadership system.

- Account plans
- Department plans
- Training plans

Do

This stage has two main steps.

1. Communicate, empower, deploy
   - All employee meetings
   - Sales connection
2. Perform to plan and measure
   - District operating plans
   - Critical PL statement
   - Balanced Scorecard

Check

This stage has two main steps.

1. Review performance
   - Group support system performance management process
   - Leadership meetings
   - Performance matrix
   - APEX review
   - Employee survey
   - Customer survey
2. Develop reward and recognize
   - Pay for performance
   - Incentive plans
   - Pinnacle club

Act

This stage has one main step.

1. Learn, innovate, and improve
   - Process review
   - Action plans
   - Business Excellence (BE) gap analysis

MANAGE PERFORMANCE

During the PDCA "Check" stage, it is required to manage the performance. This can best be achieved by following the steps of the performance improvement cycle described in Figure 2.2.

- Define organizational need/performance requirement
  - Strategic planning to enhance the performance of people, processes, products or services

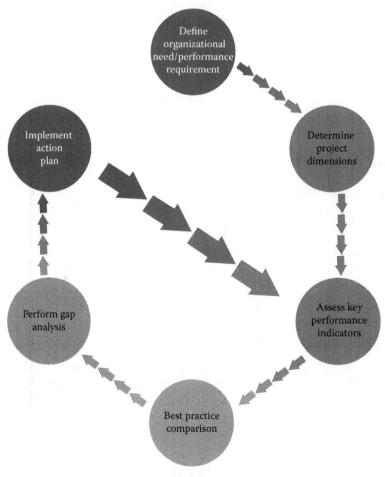

FIGURE 2.2
Performance improvement process.

- Determine project charter
  - Assess key performance indicators
- Best practice comparison
  - Benchmarking using benchmarking processes
- Perform gap analysis
- Implement action plan
- Repeat assessment cycle

The leadership system encompasses the entire Business System. The PDCA plan shows salient features of the leadership system.

The BE processes mentioned in the leadership system diagram are repeated in the Business System Framework (Table 1.2).

Let us understand LEADERSHIP components one by one.

Foundation

The senior leaders must have in place processes to communicate to all employees the following minimum leadership requirements:

Vision

Example:
"To Be the Most Admired Company in Our Markets"
To be measured by what?

Customers say:
- "We want to do more business with XYZ Organization"
Shareholders say:
- "'XYZ' is one of my best investments"
Employees say:
- "I am proud to be part of the 'XYZ' team"

Values

Example:
The organization believes that its ability to achieve its performance goals depends on its people embracing its core values:

Customer Orientation—We make our customers the focus of everything we do

People—We recognize our people as our most valued resource

Trust—We have confidence in the reliability of others to do the right thing

Respect—We treat each other with respect and consideration

Dignity—We honor the pride and self-esteem of others

Integrity—We are honest and ethical

Goals

Mission and strategy are useful concepts, but they are often too abstract for people to use on a regular basis. What is needed is a set of tools that translate mission and strategy into concepts that can be measured and understood. Top management must translate mission and strategy into metrics that we can call "Key Business Driver (KBD), Key Performance Indicator (KPI), or Vital Few."

For example: "Speedy" company can have the following vital few goals for the next year:

15% income growth
15% return on invested capital
10% sales growth
13% earnings before interest and taxes
9% free cash flow to sales

KBDs could be Safety, Quality, Speed/Delivery and Cost.

KPIs for these could be Customer defective parts per million (DPPM), Customer on-time delivery (OTD), days on hand (DOH) Inventory, Plan Adherence, and Cost Out (or cost saving). These are discussed in the assessment function and in the Balanced Scorecard.

Mission

Example:

"To be our customers' best supplier, providing distinctive and highly valued products, services and solutions."

This must be communicated to all employees through a company newspaper or by printing it on the employee badge and be part of the internal audit process.

Ethics

1. Obeying the law
2. Integrity in recording and reporting our financial results
3. Respecting human rights
4. Delivering quality
5. Competing ethically
6. Respecting diversity and fair employment practices
7. Avoiding conflicts of interest, for example, avoiding personal relationships that conflict with the organization
8. Protecting assets and information
9. Acting with integrity (avoiding bribes or kickbacks especially when selling to governments)
10. Environment, health, and safety—safeguarding health and safety of the employees and the community, and protecting the environment

Philosophy

Example:

It is our belief that we achieve excellence through our people by creating and sustaining a high-performance workplace. We drive high performance through this philosophy, which puts our core values into operations and makes us responsible to one another, to our organization, to our customers, and to other stakeholders.

Learning Organization

Many adverse situations come in the life of the organization like manufacturing slowdown or a global recession. The organization needs to stay afloat. The trick here is that this is a good time to become even more efficient through learning and acquiring useful skills. According to Professor C.K. Prahalad, the only trees that don't fall during the storm are those that have seen the draught, because their roots go very deep.

A learning organization is the organization that facilitates the learning of its employees and improves continuously by the process of improving actions through better knowledge and understanding. Learning organizations develop as a result of the challenges facing them. Constant learning enables them to remain competitive in the global business environment.

Learning organizations inspire individuals rather than calculate the number of people to fire in order to become competitive. They should be asking "how can we create the sense of purpose, possibility, and mutual commitment that will inspire ordinary individuals to feats of collective heroism?"

Lastly, creating an "unlearning organization" is just as important. "Forgetting curve is about the rate at which a company can unlearn those habits that hinder future success." Professor C.K. Prahalad (Vikalpa, 30 (2), April–June 2005 [a quarterly publication of the Indian Institute of Management, Ahmedabad, India]).

LESSONS LEARNED PROCESS

This process is mentioned in *The Tactical Guide to Six Sigma Implementation*, a sister book. It is a process to capture, document, and share lessons learned, thus infusing change in the organization.

The process answers the following questions:

- What went well?
- What could have been done differently?
- What could be improved?
- What did we do that we should not have?
- Did all our various stakeholders interact efficiently and effectively?
- Where were the gaps?
- Where were the overlaps?
- What can be done differently next time to make the situation easier for all parties involved?

The documented process promotes continued improvement and identification of additional opportunities by

- Enabling others to learn how the project/task was planned, implemented, and monitored
- Helping resolve issues
- Allowing resources to be tracked back to their work in the project
- Creating an audit trail
- Providing direction to revise or revive the project later

PUBLIC AND COMMUNITY AFFAIRS

Example:

Senior leaders need to set up processes to establish and deploy the above foundation attributes; they must additionally address the organization's public and community responsibility.

Here are the core principles of social and community responsibilities:

Protection of the Biosphere

We will reduce and make continual progress toward eliminating the release of any substance that may cause environmental damage to the air, water, or the earth.

Sustainable Use of Natural Resources

We will make sustainable use of renewable natural resources, such as water, soils, and forests. We will conserve nonrenewable natural resources through efficient use and careful planning.

Reduction and Disposal of Wastes

We will reduce and where possible eliminate waste through source reduction and recycling.

Energy Conservation

We will conserve energy and improve the energy efficiency of our internal operations and of the goods and services we sell.

Risk Reduction

We will strive to minimize the environmental, health, and safety risks to our employees and the communities in which we operate.

Safe Products and Services

We will reduce and where possible eliminate the use, manufacture, or sale of products and services that cause environmental damage or health or safety hazards. We will inform our customers of the environmental impacts of our products or services and try to correct unsafe use.

Environmental Restoration

We will promptly and responsibly correct conditions we have caused that endanger health, safety, or the environment. To the extent feasible, we will redress injuries we have caused to persons or damage we have caused to the environment and will restore the environment.

Management Commitment

We will implement these principles and sustain a process that ensures that the board of directors and chief executive officer are fully informed and are responsible for this environmental policy.

3

Strategic Planning

The pyramid in Figure 3.1 represents an organization with its core values and business drivers as a foundation and total customer satisfaction on top.

STRATEGIC PLANNING PYRAMID

Essential steps for organizational strategic plan are presented in this pyramid. Core values and market drivers form an organization's philosophy. This philosophy helps the organization determine its strategic initiatives for the goals to achieve growth for the planned period. Team and personal growth goals supported by Organizational Capability Analysis (OCA) enable all team members to achieve performance excellence (APEX). Profit plan goals are determined for the growth of the business. All metrics of the goals are pursued for the continuous improvement resulting in total customer (stakeholder) satisfaction.

FUNDAMENTAL CONCEPTS FOR STRATEGIC PLANNING

Within the Business System (BS), senior management should preferably identify five strategic concepts that are absolutely crucial to business' continued success:

- Modern business interactions
- Vision
- Growth

FIGURE 3.1
Strategic planning pyramid.

- Operational excellence
- Organizational capability

These five concepts are the foundation of the strategic plan.

MODERN BUSINESS INTERACTIONS

According to the digital technology gurus, the current world economy is all set for a sea of change in business activities. It may be recalled that barely two centuries ago, the Industrial Revolution saw dramatic changes in the economies of production and transportation. A tsunami of similar proportions is about to kick-start in the economies because of the Digital Revolution.

The key phrase is going to be transaction interactions.

TRANSACTION INTERACTIONS

Interactions shape economic activities. Take an example of a farm tractor manufacturer in the United States. With vertical integration of manufacturing processes, their interaction costs were lower within the firm, while their production (transformation) costs were higher as compared to specialist outside suppliers.

They minimized their transformation costs by buying an engine from Japan, transmission assembly from India, axle assembly from China, and body parts from Canada. The new tractor assembly line was reduced to five stations including a final test and two persons for maintenance and test drive. All was done by increasing interaction activities with the use of information technology and the Internet, which enabled them to find the lowest total transformation cost suppliers internationally.

Today, even the smallest start-up has access to a global market for its products. Take "BizChair.com" founder Sean as an example. Sean is a real entrepreneur, at 14 years old, he locked himself in his bedroom, and three days later, his business was born! Now, he is earning more than $50,000,000 a year selling business chairs online. Sean has been an inspiration to young people around the world trying to sell online!

PURCHASING POWER PARITY (PPP) AND GLOBAL MARKET

In simple words, PPP can be explained by this example: A chocolate bar that sells for Indian Rupees 65 in an Indian city should cost US$1.00 in a U.S. city when the exchange rate between India and the United States is 65 USD/INR. (Both chocolate bars cost US$1.00.)

Because of the effect of PPP, companies searching for customers will be increasingly likely to strike gold as the number of consumers earning more than $10,000 a year at purchasing power parity swells from 800 million today to almost 2.4 billion by 2025, aided by growth in developing economies such as China, India, and Indonesia.

VISION (STRATEGIC PLANNING)

Vision is your market vision. This section should describe both what the market leader will be doing better than the competition and what your business will need to be that market leader. Your market vision is not a tag line—a slogan, but addresses questions such as the following:

What will the competitive landscape of your industry look like in five–ten years?

What will market forces require you to do? What will they allow you to do? What will our customers reward? What won't they?

Describe why a shift in scale, technology, global presence, and systems orientation will produce greater value for your customers and shareholders.

Describe your business environment in five to ten years. What major opportunities and risks will you face in this environment?

This topic represents the most important aspect of your business strategy and should demonstrate a clear stance on the external market forces and trends that will shape your competitive environment over the planning horizon and beyond. This topic provides you with a vehicle to present your outlook of what your business and industry will look like in one to five years. Once presented, this vision sets the stage for the remainder of your strategy.

In building your position on the evolution of your market and competitive landscape, you may broaden your outlook to consider all attractive market opportunities. This effort will present new markets, customers, technologies, applications, and competitors. Along with those opportunities and risks, there will be other issues that might surface if the traditional "rules of the game" that define today's industries were challenged. Consistent with your focus on innovation, you will likely expand your analysis to include paradigms that, while currently unproven, may eventually become the norm.

While you should identify and speak to those external forces that are expected to most closely affect your particular environment, potential items for consideration in addressing this topic may include the following:

1. Changing customer needs
2. Threat of new entrants

3. Strategies customers are pursuing
4. Shifting economic trends
5. Power shifts in the supply chain
6. Expected technological changes
7. Regulatory and political factors
8. Developments in global markets
9. Strategies competitors are pursuing
10. Trends in distribution practices
11. Rising trends in the supplier base
12. Rising cost and pricing pressures
13. Incongruities (e.g., growing markets with falling profits)
14. Overall industry shifts
15. Demographic changes

In terms of a mission or vision statement, you will want to ensure at whatever organizational level you are planning at—Group, Operation, Division, Business Unit—that you maintain linkage to your corporate mission statement. The power of unity is in that connection to a common mission and your planning efforts are best spent on describing your market.

Having established the market vision, Lean Six Sigma linkage is used to determine the process, inputs (Key Performance Indicators), and outputs (Key Business Drivers) for

- Growth
- Operational excellence
- Organizational capability

Figure 3.3 shows how Lean Six Sigma (LSS) links Key Performance Indicators to Key Business Drivers resulting in value creation for the customer for these three.

GROWTH (STRATEGIC PLANNING)

It is your path to market leadership. Given your market vision, growth plots the course of your business to its value maximizing position in the industry. In plotting that course, your assessment of customer wants, competitor activities, and technological shifts will come into play just as much as which systems or solutions you are offering and which new products or services you will launch over the next five years. This component of your plan should perform the scenario analysis necessary to show the pros and cons of alternative approaches. This section should explore any breakout opportunities to leap ahead of the competitive pack.

Describe how you will position your business to take fullest advantage of these opportunities. Define a reaching, credible, and enduring strategy for global leadership. Why have you selected this strategy over other alternatives? Why are you convinced that this is the winning strategy?

Given your vision for the competitive landscape, the growth section allows you to detail the strategy you believe will most effectively capitalize on the opportunities that you will face within that environment. In one sense, this section provides your organization (and its relevant stakeholders) with a firm understanding of what you intend to do with your business and where you intend to take it.

Current resources and bottlenecks should not limit the creative thinking of your operation. The emphasis should be on your operation's potential … not its current position.

As you address this component, consider the following questions that are consistent with BS to trigger other subjects that may be more relevant to your operation's particular situation.

How will you achieve at least 10% average annual sales and earnings growth?

How will you generate at least a top-quartile, greater than 9% free cash flow?

What markets, segments, customers, applications, and geographic regions will you target? Which offers the highest growth opportunities? Which global markets are best for your business? What new products will you develop? What current offerings will you discontinue?

What will your technology roadmap look like?

How does your unit contribute to next year's corporate goals?

Will you market to the same customers that you do today? Will you utilize the same suppliers? Will you have the same competitors? Should you continue to do business with these groups in the future? How will the way you do business with them change?

What aspects of E-Business can accelerate your growth curve or improve the probability of achieving your plan?

OPERATIONAL EXCELLENCE (STRATEGIC PLANNING)

It addresses the capital and process management to fuel your growth. Operational excellence presents your plan, at a strategic level, to sustain profitability, to increase your productivity, and to build a competitive advantage valued by your market. While the focus is broader than cost reduction, the value of this aspect of your strategy manifests itself by satisfying the need for capital to fuel growth and achieve the leadership position outlined by your vision.

How will you respond to finance your growth plan and assure ongoing top-tier returns? How much cost will you need to take out of your enterprise? Which aspects of your operations are ahead of the competition? What will customers demand going forward?

Operational excellence and cost out activities are critical components to ensuring your business can meet the demands of growing into the leadership position defined by your market vision. You will likely need your functional leaders to work with other operating and functional leaders to ensure connectivity of the strategic issues and the resolution.

As you address this component, consider the following questions that are consistent with the BS. Again, this listing is not exhaustive; please use it to trigger other subjects that may be more relevant to your operation's particular situation.

- How will you finance the targeted growth?
- How will you improve productivity 4% (at least) annually?
- How will you improve supplier resource management?
- What products need to be designed for lower cost?
- How are you driving cross-unit cost reduction programs such as supplier resource management?
- What is the goal for reducing the cost of nonconformance?
- What specific performance recovery programs are you driving?
- What aspects of E-Business can accelerate your growth curve or improve the probability of achieving your plan?

ORGANIZATIONAL CAPABILITY

It describes the viability of your business' human capital to execute your strategy. All businesses demand a high-performance, accountable, results-oriented culture. The focus is on the strategic ramifications of human capability in your organization, not the demographics or day-to-day culture. Organizational Capability Analysis (OCA) is discussed in detail later in this chapter.

Where do you stand in terms of having the human capital and organizational architecture to achieve your strategy?

The focus of organizational capability is on the strategic issues that reflect your human capital, its performance, capacity, and structure, ensuring the successful execution of the business' strategy. The focus is really on the first question shown below—plans to align strategy, capability, organization, and compensation. Again, your functional leaders in this area may need to coordinate heavily with corporate and other operating executives to maximize the impact of this part of your strategic plan. In essence, what emanates from this assessment is a strategic human resources plan that is highly compatible with the business' strategy and a principal enabler of bringing the business strategy to fruition.

As you address this component, consider the following questions that are consistent with BS. Again, this listing is not exhaustive; please use it to trigger other subjects that may be more relevant to your operation's particular situation.

- How will you align your organization's strategy, competencies, leadership team, organization structure, communications processes, and reward systems?
- What specific change(s) will you need to drive, to build, and to sustain an organizational culture that will enable you to realize your strategy?
- How will you effect the necessary changes?

PLAN STAGES, GATES, AND REQUIRED RESOURCES

A Gantt chart or a project planning tool for implementing your plan should address the sequencing of events, major decision points, and necessary resources to achieve success. These points (stages, gates, and resources) are critical to developing, communicating, and measuring your strategic plan. Table 3.1 explains plan stages, gates, key activities for each gate and required considerations and resources.

OBJECTIVES DEVELOPMENT

How do you collect and analyze relevant data and information to address these factors as they relate to your planning process? Here is how.

Through the following activities:

- Customer data obtained through divisional product management and sales team
- Listen and learn
- Surveys
- Competitive environment study through sales team
- Technological changes through Engineering Change Order (ECO)/ Marketing Product Specification (MPS) and divisional engineering
- Strengths and weaknesses through Quality Operating System (QOS) process and functional SWOT
- Supplier/Partner Strength, Weakness, Opportunity, and Threat (SWOT) via QOS and Supply Chain Management (SCM) visits

What are your key objectives?

Below is an example of the objectives for a five-year term.

Current Focus (each objective is shown in a different shade)
- Objective 1—Delivery
- Objective 2—Customer focused
- Objective 3—Quality

Forward Looking
- Objective 4—60% manifold (block for assembling control devices) in-sourcing
- Objective 5—Five-axis CNC machining

Objectives development "fix, focus, and flex" (example)

Table 3.2 shows an example for a five-year plan for organizational objectives.

Quarterly objectives development

These objectives need to be converted into goals, each goal having its own metric.

TABLE 3.1

Plan Stages, Gates, and Required Resource Considerations

Stages	Key Activities at Each Gate	Key Considerations and Resources
Concept	• Identify, develop, and assess alternative business and technical concepts • Develop preliminary business plan • Develop preliminary project plan	• Realistic and achievable forecasts • Financial attractiveness • Realistic and achievable projects plans • Feasible product concept • Resources availability • Acceptable project risk
Definition	• Finalize business plan • Finalize project requirements and specifications • Develop preliminary manufacturing plan • Identify capital requirements • Develop comprehensive project plan	• Acceptable business and project plans • Design feasibility • Capital requirements • Product and project risks
Design and development	• Engineering release and design verification • Finalize manufacturing process design • Finalize equipment tooling and gauging capital requirements • Develop market launch plans	• Design verification results • Sales and marketing support readiness • Interim quality plan approvals • Product and project risks
Validation	• Install all production processes, equipment tooling, and gauges • Execute production trial run • Perform process capability study • Perform validation testing	• Validation results • Sales and marketing support readiness • Process capability • Product and project risks
Production	• Product/Part Approval Process (PPAP) submitted and approved • Limited line rate production • Customer satisfaction tracking	• PPAP approvals • Product cost versus targets • Distribution channel readiness
Audit	• Full line rate production • Metrics monitoring • Customer satisfaction tracking • Capture lessons learned	• Customer feedback • Project performance versus business plan

TABLE 3.2

A Five-Year Plan for Objectives—Example

Fix		Focus	Flex	
2006	2007	2008	2009	2010
Fix delivery time issues through SIOP and Pull System to improve Customer On-Time Delivery (OTD)	Enhance Customer Satisfaction: OTD > 95%	Leverage SIOP OTD > 95%	Leverage SIOP OTD > 96%	Leverage SIOP OTD > 97%
Build robust supplier partnerships through increased MRP communication	Increase distribution mix >33% by increasing the depth and breadth of the product velocity program	Drastic reduction in lead times	Drastic reduction in lead times	Drastic reduction in lead times
		LSS score > 4.2	LSS score > 4.5	LSS score > 4.5
		Full Supplier-viz Software Implementation	World Class Customer Responsiveness	World Class Customer Responsiveness
Supplement our cultural strengths by full implementation of MESH, PWP, and QOS	Sustain "World Class" safety levels while integrating machining operations	Benchmark in safety and floor-driven QOS/ GQMS Culture/MESH/ PWP cascading to lower levels of organization	Benchmark in safety and floor-driven QOS/ GQMS Culture/MESH/ PWP	Benchmark in safety and floor-driven QOS/ GQMS Culture/MESH/ PWP
Benchmark in employee engagement and empowerment while protecting the safety of our associates and having a positive impact in our community	Improve the well-being and satisfaction of our employees through Hydraulic Benchmark performance in MESH, PWP, and GQMS/ QOS		All employee involvement	All employee involvement

(Continued)

TABLE 3.2 (CONTINUED)

A Five-Year Plan for Objectives—Example

	Fix		Focus		Flex	
	2006	2007	2008	2009	2009	2010
	Become the quality leader in our markets through process excellence, GQMS implementation, and ISO-TS 16949 certification	Become the benchmark in quality in our market Improve our quality through DPPM reduction and GQMS Continue driving the Lean journey and cell-based culture for CNC five-axis machining center	Double-digit DPPMs Process Quality > 4.2 Sigma	Double-digit DPPMs Process Quality > 4.3 Sigma		Double-digit DPPMs Process Quality > 4.5 Sigma
	Create a culture that every associate feels like the owner of our business and actively contributes to driving toward 15% operating profit in 2009	Partnership with SCM to hit 2007 cost out target Utilization of LSS principles to reduce DOH and drive down internal cost and supplier cost	15% OI 25% Standard margin >4% Productivity	15% OI 25% Standard margin >4% Productivity		

TABLE 3.3

Quarterly Objectives Development

Plant Operations	Description	Goal
Achieve financial performance	Free cash flow (FCF)	9.0%
	Operating profit ($M)	$0.24
	Operating profit as % sales	2.4%
	Achieve cost outs ($,000)	$3183
	Improve DOH and inventory $	XX/$7.8 m
	Meet capital spend plan per quarter plan	$212
	SOX compliance—risk mitigation	No med/high
Operational excellence	Improve delivery performance	95% by Q4
	Reduce past dues ($,000) by 50%	<$250K
	Customer DPPM	513
	Warranty reduction	Improve 15%
	Scrap reduction—% of sales	1.0%
	Variable mfg expense as % of direct labor	1248%
	GQMS implementation	>90%
	Achieve BE certification score	>500
	MESH implementation—external certify	85%
	Reduce recordable incident rate	0.2
	LSS score—improve culture focus	3.5—Q2
		4.3—Q4
Growth	5-Axis machining strategy for MCDs	Proposal 1Q07
Organizational capability and culture	Complete OCA plans—mid-talent upgrade	Per timing
	Employee engagement—survey score	10% improve
	Diversity + new hires	30%
	APEX implementation	100%
	Validated PWP assessment	2.5

These metrics are reviewed every quarter for continuous improvement. Table 3.3 shows an example.

IMPORTANT BS COMPONENTS FOR STRATEGIC PLANNING

- Profit plan
- OCA
- APEX

PROFIT PLAN

As shown in Figure 3.1, profit plan is one of the most important aspects of the BS. Profit planning is supported by four concepts, namely, marketing vision, growth, operational excellence, and organizational capability. It has three main components.

1. Understanding the inputs, processes, and outputs for each one of the four concepts of the business system and leveraging the process outputs to determine the profit plan

   Figure 3.2 shows four concepts of profit plan—their inputs, processes, and outputs.
2. Profit plan linkage to Lean Six Sigma for operational excellence

   Figure 3.3 shows profit plan linkage to LSS for operational excellence.
3. Zero-based budgeting for profit planning

   Budget is the result of a sound profit planning. It states the organization's plan, which provides objective planning as well as control.

   Generally, firms take a typical budgeting approach. The previous year's budget is taken as a base and expenses are added to it according to anticipated needs. This yearly incremental approach to budgeting is also called rolling budgets. Here, in incremental budgeting, business managers justify only increases over the previous year's budget and very little attention is paid to new projects, innovative methods, or efficient equipment.

   Zero-based budgeting provides a better alternative. It is a method that helps and promotes efficient and strategic planning, which helps in better decision making for the business. It starts with a management review of each department's purpose and goals. All proposed expenses go through an approval process rather than the approval of only the increments.

   After a new project or new marketing campaign is identified, the additional funding resources to complete the task are planned.

   For example, if an existing expense of newspaper advertising for the last few years does not increase the market share you expected, you must review it immediately and decide where those funds should be spent, in television and radio advertising or in Internet marketing, or whether they should not be spent at all.

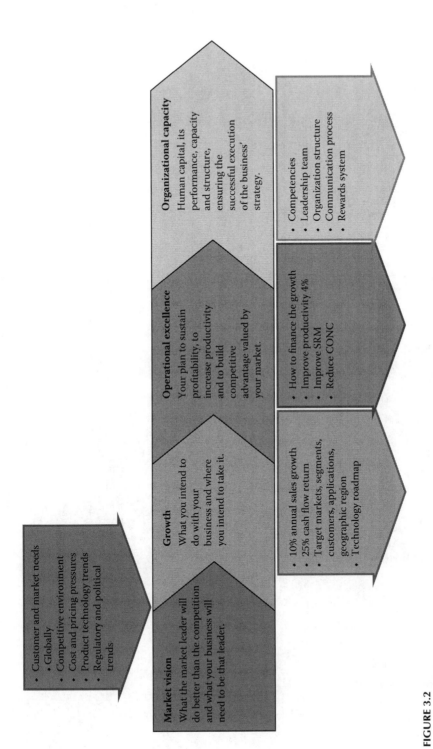

FIGURE 3.2
Four concepts of profit plan—their inputs and outputs.

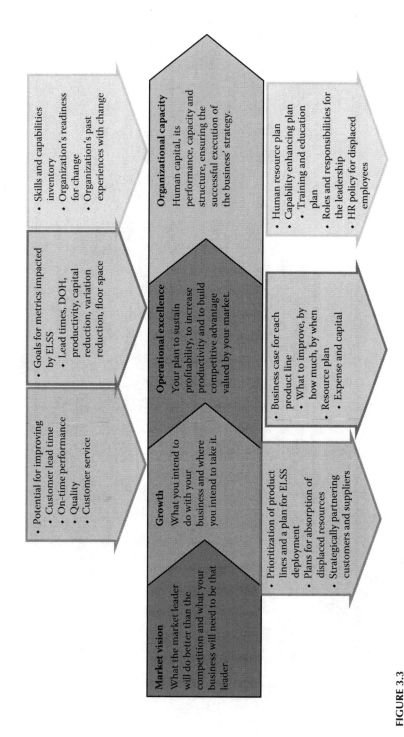

FIGURE 3.3

Linkage of Lean Six Sigma to strategic planning.

The zero-based budget requires you to lay out a sales plan, a profit plan, and what you need to achieve a profit. The following steps are a must for a good zero-based budget.

1. Itemize your fixed costs like mortgage, rent, utilities, fixed salaries, supplies, and outsourced services.
2. Brainstorm these expense items to the correct base needed, not just what you spent last year, and then implement a savings and expense control plan by taking tough decisions.
3. Your variable costs should fluctuate on a needs basis depending on your projects, sales plan, and a new market or new product plan.
4. Develop your sales plan on the basis of minimum sales to cover your fixed and variable costs. Once you have developed this base plan and your minimum breakeven points for daily, monthly, and yearly profits, you will create an internal organizational desire to remain above the breakeven point and contribute to higher profits.
5. Publish sales plans versus cost plans to show breakeven and profit centers for each project.

ORGANIZATIONAL CAPABILITY ANALYSIS (OCA)

Objectives of the OCA

- Develop current employees
- Expecting and coaching for high performance, not tolerating low performance
- Taking and creating opportunities to upgrade by hiring top performers
- Aggressively identifying and developing future leaders of the corporation with broad experiences
- Driving the organization's Leadership Model for excellence in leadership

Business Excellence Leadership Model and Supporting Competencies:
Table 3.4 shows how the leadership model and competencies fit together. The following are the four leadership classes considered:

1. Executives and VPs
2. Unit/department managers

TABLE 3.4

Leadership Attributes Required for OCA

	Leadership Competencies (Executives and VPs)	Frontline Leader Competencies (Managers)	Individual Contributor Competencies (Supervisors)	Admin Support and Technician (Individual Contributor Competencies)
Thinks and acts strategically	• Business acumen • Vision and purpose • Intellectual rigor	• Business acumen • Vision and purpose • Intellectual rigor	• Makes decisions/solves problems	• Makes decisions/solves problems
Gets results	• Drive for results • Change and adaptability • Leveraging resources	• Drive for results • Change and adaptability • Leveraging resources	• Drive for results • Promotes and champions changes	• Drive for results • Promotes and champions changes
Builds organizational capability	• Managerial courage • Holding self/others accountable • Developing and motivating others	• Managerial courage • Holding self/others accountable • Developing and motivating others	• Pursues personal development	• Pursues personal development
Demonstrates leadership style	• Interpersonal communication skills • Professional presence	• Interpersonal communication skills • Professional presence	• Demonstrates a collaborative style	• Demonstrates a collaborative style

3. Supervisors
4. Administrative individual contributors

The nomenclature of the competencies required by each class is the same, but within that competency, each class has different levels of competencies. For example, the competency "Thinks and acts strategically" for VPs means business acumen, and so on, but for supervisors, it means "Makes decisions and solves problems."

Leadership Attributes and Competencies Required for OCA

Table 3.4 shows leadership attributes and competencies required for OCA. Competencies for

1. Leadership (executives and VPs)
2. Frontline leader (managers)
3. Individual contributor (supervisors)
4. Admin support and technician individual contributor

Four Attributes of the Leadership required for each category:

- Thinks and acts strategically
- Gets results
- Builds organizational capability
- Demonstrates leadership style

Leadership Competencies (Executives and VPs)

Thinks and Acts Strategically

Possesses Business Acumen, Intellectual Rigor, Vision, and Purpose

- Sees the big picture and demonstrates analytical and creative thinking when creating plans and solving problems
- Establishes and implements effective strategies and measures effectiveness
- Works toward the company's long-term success as well as for own business'/function's short-term success
- Sees the big picture, understands and considers customers, competitors, markets, industry, and so on, when making plans and decisions

- Demonstrates an understanding of the broader organization, and how their role or function fits into the strategic plan and overall direction of the company
- Strategically positions their function or business to align with the company's strategy
- Demonstrates strong intellectual capability and analytical smarts, is able to distill complex issues into workable pieces, and can take all of the information from looking at the "big picture," make sense of it, and develop plans from it
- Establishes and implements effective strategies, measures effectiveness, has strong business and financial acumen, and understands all segments (i.e., front end and operations) and how they interact
- Demonstrates creative thinking, brings creativity to plans and decisions, and finds new, innovative ways, where appropriate

Gets Results

Ready to Change, Adapt, and Drive for Results by Leveraging Resources
Consistently meets and exceeds expectations and understands that "how" accomplishments are achieved is as important as "what" is actually achieved.

- Does not undermine others for personal gain
- Has a strategy for driving change and is able to bring focus and purpose to the work objectives for others
- Effectively delegates to adapt to changing business priorities
- Can get others on board, remains engaged and committed to objectives, and can overcome resistance
- Can manage the support structure necessary to drive business objectives and pulls the key levers of structure, processes, HR practices, metrics, and rewards to execute strategy and objectives
- Runs a profitable business

Builds Organizational Capability

- Demonstrates a commitment to power-of-one as it relates to talent development by proactively moving talent out of their organization into the organization's other groups/departments, and moving talent into their organization from other groups/departments
- Optimizes utilization of HR assets and allocates human capital to the most impactful and value-added activities

- Seeks out new talent from different backgrounds, cultures, and experiences, and actively values diversity
- Is able to select, assess, and develop talent; hires ahead of the growth curve; doesn't hire for current position only; considers assessment and selection of A players
- Raises the performance bar—creates, promotes, and sustains a performance culture
- Creates alignment so that everyone within the organization knows the strategy
- Designs/restructures the organization to achieve business results
- Drives differentiated reviews and feedback; establishes open, candid, and trusting relationships
- Treats others fairly and consistently
- Is good at experience-based development, providing key talent, fresh and challenging assignments; coaching

Demonstrates a Leadership Style

- Lives and embodies the company values and philosophies
- Actively drives and lives the BS
- Projects an exemplary executive image with polish, poise, professionalism, and integrity
- Sets an example of open, honest, timely, and persuasive communication; communication style is approachable and instills trust and confidence
- Makes and supports decisions based on ethics, honesty, and fairness
- Acts in the best interests of the company and its stakeholders (employees, customers, and shareholders); accepts the role of leadership as a 24/7 responsibility
- Inspires others to action
- Is respectful of cultural and organizational norms; is able to adjust style, message, or behavior as needed
- Effectively handles conflicts and issues affecting working relationships
- Lives up to commitments made to employees, colleagues, and customers
- Acts as an ambassador of the company; is actively involved within the communities in which the company does business with
- Works collaboratively and openly across boundaries/business lines; leverages resources; willingly shares information and relevant resource

Frontline Leader Competencies (Managers)

Thinks and Acts Strategically
- Demonstrates an understanding of the broader organization, and how their role or function fits into the strategic plan and overall direction of the company
- Ensures their department/site/function understands and supports both their business/function's strategy and how it fits into the company's vision of being an integrated operating company
- Sees the big picture; considers trends with customers, competitors, suppliers, markets, industries, and so on when making plans and decisions
- Uses analytical abilities to distill complex issues into workable/meaningful parts for themselves and others
- Demonstrates creative thinking; brings creativity to plans and decisions; finds new, innovative ways where appropriate
- Makes data-based decisions NOT based on opinion or anecdote

Gets Results
- Effectively models, manages, and drives change; engages/builds commitment to changes
- Can get others on board, engaged, and committed to objectives; can overcome resistance
- Effectively gets things done through others by delegating, motivating, focusing, and leveraging the appropriate resources to meet objectives
- Does not undermine others for personal gain
- Sustains focus on critical objectives throughout the entire cycle
- Develops own skills in order to consistently meet objectives and targets
- Drives compliance to the ethics policy and holds others accountable for ethical conduct—ensures results and high performance is not sought "at any cost," putting ethics at risk

Builds Organizational Capability
- Demonstrates a commitment to One Company as it relates to talent development by proactively moving talent out of their organization into other company groups and moving talent into their organization from other company groups
- Seeks out new talent from different backgrounds, cultures, and experiences—actively values diversity

- Proactively plans for new resources/skill sets/requirements based on changing business needs
- Accurately identifies "top talent" within their organization and among external candidates; can "calibrate" talent
- Raises the performance bar—creates, promotes, and sustains a performance culture; ensures employees continuously raise the bar on their own performance
- Creates alignment so that everyone within the organization knows the business objectives
- Performance reviews are timely, thoughtful, and impactful, resulting in differentiated evaluations and rewards
- Treats others fairly and consistently
- Is effective at experience-based development, providing key talent, fresh and challenging assignments; coaching
- Behaves in accordance with expressed beliefs and commitments
- Identifies and manages underperformers effectively and expeditiously
- Takes active leadership in employee communications—effective in one-on-one (coaching) as well as in group meetings

Demonstrates a Leadership Style
- Lives and embodies the company values and philosophies—manages with respect and fairness; assists employees in taking responsibility for their own performance, behavior, and growth
- Actively drives and lives the BS
- Projects an exemplary leadership image with polish, poise, professionalism, and integrity
- Is approachable and instills trust and credibility with others
- Acts in the best interests of the company and its stakeholders (employees, customers, and shareholders); accepts the role of leadership as a 24/7 responsibility
- Inspires others to action
- Is respectful of cultural and organizational norms; is able to adjust style, message, or behavior as needed
- Effectively handles conflicts and issues affecting working relationships
- Lives up to commitments made to employees, colleagues, and customers
- Acts as an ambassador of the company; is actively involved within the communities in which the company does business with
- Works collaboratively across boundaries/business lines and openly shares information and resources

Individual Contributor Competencies (Supervisors)

Thinks and Acts Strategically

- Keeps current with information and technology—Seeks available learning opportunities to improve skills and knowledge of relevant issues—customers, products, operations technology, and financial indicators—to facilitate understanding and utilization of the metrics on the Balanced Scorecard and broaden business perspective
- Understands overall business performance—Demonstrates understanding of the factors that affect short-term business results and educates employees to create understanding about the impact of each individual on the organization's performance
- Seeks to understand customers—Actively seeks information to understand internal and external customers' circumstances, problems, expectations, and needs, and shares customer information with employees to build understanding
- Communicates vision—Translates and reinforces the group vision and the local business plan into understandable terms for employees, and links day-to-day individual and group activities to plan outcomes
- Interprets new concepts—Grasps new or unfamiliar concepts quickly, breaking down a situation or problem into meaningful components that can be communicated effectively at all levels
- Practices continuous learning—Seeks new ideas, perspectives, and approaches and applies learnings from past experiences and education to current situation

Gets Results

- Drives continuous improvement—Strives for continuous improvement in process and business results; actively seeks alternative solutions and recognizes problems as opportunities for process improvement
- Challenges status quo—Continually challenges current thinking regarding people and process and recommends changes to improve operations; encourages individuals to constructively question established work processes or assumptions
- Manages personal change—Treats change and new situations as opportunities for learning and growth; focuses on the beneficial aspects of change by helping employees identify the benefits to them personally; helps individuals overcome resistance to change; shows empathy with those who resist or fear change

- Demonstrates personal drive—Is self-disciplined; frequently measures progress and evaluates results; reprioritizes and develops action plans to improve progress of goals as appropriate; prevents irrelevant issues or distractions from interfering with timely completion of important tasks
- Applies business tools—Applies prescribed BS tools such as Lean Systems, Six Sigma, Employee Survey Action Plans, and so on, to improve organizational effectiveness
- Sets high standards—For their organization to continuously raise the expectations and standards that define success
- Gains cross boundary support—Works across the organization to provide resources to other departments and foster collaboration to ensure business goals are met
- Aligns and prioritizes resources—Utilizes appropriate processes, equipment, and human resources required to meet organizational and department goals; focuses time, energy, and resources on the most critical activities
- Builds effective working relationships—Proactively builds effective working relationships between one's area and other areas, teams, departments, units, or organizations to help achieve business goals

Builds Organizational Capability
- Addresses difficult performance issues—Takes appropriate action to improve performance to meet expectations; addresses substandard performance through actionable performance feedback and applies appropriate performance improvement actions, up to and including termination
- Communicates difficult messages—Effectively delivers unpopular messages, which helps create understanding and acceptance; handles difficult situations effectively, providing candid, corrective feedback to address issues
- Stands alone—Willingness to take stands that may be unpopular and provide feedback to more senior managers that is contrary to ideas or accepted practices
- Manages work—Establishes clear directions, lays out work in a well-planned and organized manner, and assigns clear responsibility for tasks
- Provides performance feedback—Provides ongoing coaching and feedback on employee performance, reinforcing positive behaviors

and providing guidance to correct performance that is not meeting expectations

- Manages performance—Applies performance management skills and company policies to effectively motivate people to high performance, sets clear performance standards, and holds people accountable for results; develops and maintains performance metrics as required to monitor results and uses as a tool to identify and initiate process improvements
- Ensures safe work environment—Proactively implements, promotes, and maintains a safe working environment through leading by example, anticipating potential accidents and taking corrective actions before incidents, to assure a safe and healthful workplace
- Provide stretch assignments—Challenges employees to learn new skills and gain experiences that will help them reach their potential
- Provides skills and tools—Ensures that employees have the necessary skills, knowledge, resources, and tools to do their jobs safely and effectively
- Promotes inclusion—Demonstrates an appreciation for similarities and individual differences by promoting a culture of inclusion that leverages the full potential of all employees
- Reinforces positive behaviors—Recognizes individual strengths and positive performance; shares ownership and visibility for individual and group success, and accepts responsibility for failures
- Enables employee involvement—Involves others in decisions, problem solving, and continuous improvement activities as appropriate
- Assesses and selects talent—Partners with HR in the assessment, selection, and promotion of employees using company guidelines and policies
- Rewards and recognizes employees—Seeks opportunities to personally recognize and celebrate the achievements of others by linking rewards and recognition to standards of excellence and business performance

Demonstrates a Leadership Style

- Builds trust and credibility—Acts as an employee advocate in appropriate situations by raising and addressing employee issues and considering employee interests and their well-being when making decisions that affect them

- Effectively communicates—Provides relevant information in a timely manner with direct reports, peers, and superiors, and is proficient in both written and oral communications
- Actively listens—Encourages others to express opinions and actively listens to understand others. Consistently practices "open door" philosophy by being approachable at all times and stressing personal, face-to-face communications
- Influences others—Communicates differing perspectives in ways that move others to action or to change one's views
- Professional demeanor—Maintains a balance between professional and personal relationships with one's employees and interacts appropriately with all levels
- Presentation skills—Organizes thoughts before communicating and tailors/modifies the message based on audience expectations to effectively present/articulate ideas, to both formal and informal groups
- Meeting leadership—Plans and runs well-organized meetings, demonstrating meeting process and facilitation skills
- Self-management—Maintains composure at all times and encourages others to do the same; stays focused and handles difficult situations effectively
- Personal presence—Presents a positive image to those inside and outside the company; behaves in a professional manner, consistent with the company philosophy and ethics policy
- Role model—Is consistent and fair when dealing with people; honors personal commitments and models company philosophy values in personal interactions

Administrative Support and Technician Individual Contributor Competencies

Makes Decisions/Solves Problems

- Makes effective decisions, even when dealing with limited or ambiguous information
- Breaks down complex problems into manageable components to better identify the root cause of the problem
- Makes well-informed and effective decisions/recommendations for addressing problems/opportunities within own area of responsibility

- Involves and informs others, as appropriate in identifying issues, problems, opportunities, and developing solutions
- Thinks issues through, anticipates problems, and takes action to prevent them or minimize their impact
- Develops innovative/creative approaches to problems/opportunities that achieve desired outcome
- Considers multiple factors (e.g., internal/external customer requirements, time constraints, costs, and desired outcomes) when making recommendations/decisions
- Follows up with colleagues/team members to ensure that the agreed upon action/decision is completed by colleagues/team members

Drives for Results

- Strives to go beyond what is expected
- Assumes personal accountability
- Takes quick, decisive action to capitalize on opportunities, minimize potential problems, and accomplish goals
- Takes initiative; does all that should be done, not just as directed or required by job description
- Takes responsibility for own decisions, actions, and results; accepts blame and shares credit, when appropriate
- Demonstrates enthusiasm and a willingness to take on new challenges, responsibilities, and assignments
- Works with a sense of urgency to complete projects or tasks within budget and on time, meeting or exceeding customer's expectations
- Prioritizes more critical and less critical activities and tasks
- Organizes and schedules self and resources to ensure completion of projects and tasks
- Uses effective methods for storing and retrieving important information
- Effectively plans, organizes, tracks, and follows up on multiple priorities

Promotes and Champions Change

- Willingly changes direction or behavior in response to changing priorities
- Adapts style to be appropriate for each situation
- Remains productive during periods of ambiguity, uncertainty, and change

- Is flexible and adaptable; changes own activities with little notice; is prepared for change as the department's priorities change
- Demonstrates support of a change by being able to communicate the what, why, and how behind the change, as well as the impact on key stakeholders (e.g., customers, team members, and department)

Pursues Personal Development

- Quickly masters new or unfamiliar concepts needed to perform effectively
- Actively seeks out development activities to enhance job, improve skills, add value, and increase knowledge
- Regularly reviews strengths and weaknesses and develops plans to build and strengthen abilities needed for success on the job
- Asks for feedback from others (manager, peers, professional network, and other team members) to enhance self-insight and job performance
- Seeks manager's advice, support, and coaching on development plans
- Takes ownership for personal development by creating development plan and following through on developmental actions and commitments

Demonstrates a Collaborative Style

- Presents ideas and facts clearly and effectively in writing (e.g., e-mails, reports, and customer correspondence) and demonstrates a strong professional image
- Effectively communicates (orally) facts, ideas, opinions, or concerns with people at all levels in the organization (peers, team members, senior management, etc.)
- Instills trust and confidence; is open, honest, and approachable
- Behaves in accordance with the beliefs and commitments expressed in the company philosophy
- Projects a professional image in appearance, communication, and behavior
- Maintains composure during times of stress; acts appropriately in good times and bad
- Collaborates and cooperates with team members/colleagues to accomplish shared goals; supports others when requested
- Promptly and completely responds to requests and provides information and resources to other teams, functions, or business units
- Effectively plans, prepares for, and conducts meetings

Important Note: It may be observed that as you go down the management levels, the content of the number attributes in each category goes up. This is a proof of the strategic belief that an organization becomes strong through its competent workforce.

The Performance Assessment

The performance assessment is carried out on two fronts:

- Accomplishments ratings
- Leadership competency ratings

Accomplishments Ratings

"O"—**Outstanding** completion of job responsibilities. Extraordinary accomplishments and results against goals. "Setting the bar" for others.

"H"—**Highly effective** in fulfilling job responsibilities. Considering the degree of difficulty of goals, resources available, and changes throughout the year, excelled in accomplishments.

"P"—**Performing** well in fulfilling job responsibilities and finds ways to "raise the bar" on (continuously improve) own performance AND considering the degree of difficulty of goals, resources available, and changes throughout the year, accomplishments against goals were fully satisfactory.

"N"—**Needs improvement** in meeting ongoing job responsibilities and improvement needed in results and accomplishments. May be responsive but needs to increase initiative and find ways to continuously improve. Should be able to improve with coaching, feedback, and an improvement plan.

"U"—**Unsatisfactory:** Significant gaps in fulfilling job requirements or achieving results. Immediate and sustained improvement required.

Leadership/Competency Ratings

On a Scale of 1 To 5

"1"—**Low Problematic**

Is not demonstrating capability, or perhaps contrary behaviors are observed. Behaviors hinder overall results/performance—a shortfall of this individual.

"2"—**Inconsistent Demonstration**

"3"—Fully Demonstrating

Understands the organization's high expectations and consistently demonstrates proficiency/effectiveness. Actively works to further develop the skills and behaviors required to "raise the bar" on their own performance.

"4"—Very Proficient

"5"—High Demonstration Role Model

Is seen as a role model; demonstrates mastery of the associated skills, competencies, and knowledge; is frequently considered a benchmark for others to emulate and learn from. Generally sets the bar for others.

ACHIEVING PERFORMANCE EXCELLENCE (APEX)

APEX Process

Figure 3.4 depicts the process for APEX.

APEX is an important business process to drive high performance throughout the organization and hold all employees accountable for delivering top performance. This process ensures effective performance management through the following four phases.

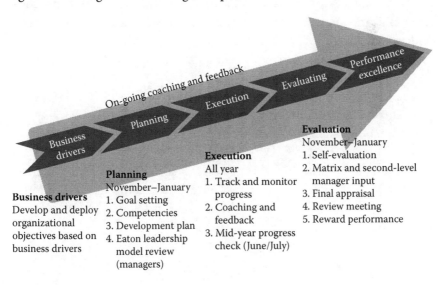

FIGURE 3.4

Process for achieving performance excellence.

Planning: It includes the following:

1. Goal setting
2. Competencies
3. Development plan
4. Leadership model

This is where commitment and ownership of the performance are built. Here, employees ask, "What is the organization striving for? How can I contribute to its success in my role? What skills and competencies do I need to make this contribution? At this stage, the employee and the manager work to establish goals and agree on competencies. The development needs to achieve these competencies are established and both of them commit to meeting the goals and exceeding the expectations.

Business Drivers: We discussed the examples of business drivers above in objectives development for strategic planning. Here, employees ask, "What must I accomplish so that I can raise the bar of my performance to a higher level?" This kind of approach aligns employees to work for their unit's success and ultimately to the organization's success.

Execution: This is where the progress on goals is tracked and coaching and feedback are provided to ensure continuous improvement in performance. Here, the employee asks, "Am I on the right track to meet my goals and performance expectations? What can I do to raise the level of my contribution? The manager asks, "How can I help you to succeed?" Here, a midyear progress check is required.

Evaluation: This is where multiple inputs are required:

- The employee's self-assessment
- Direct manager's assessment
- Functional manager's assessment

Here, employees ask, "How did I do against my goals? Has my contribution exceeded as per the expectation of the organization?" Here, the manager needs to use judgment to differentiate, recognize, and reward the levels of performance.

Quick Tips to Improve Goal Setting

Table 3.5 gives quick tips to improve goal setting.

TABLE 3.5

Quick Tips to Improve Goal Setting

Issue/Problem	Examples	How to Improve
The goal is activity based rather than result oriented.	**Activity based:** Train 3 Black Belts. **Result based:** Remove 3 calendar weeks from work process by Q1. **Result based:** Reduce order processing cycle time by 25% by the end of Q2.	Ensure the goal describes the value-added result of these actions: • Who is the customer of these actions? • What does the customer need from these actions? • If all actions are done well, what is left behind? • Why are the actions being done? • If this task/project is successful, how will the organization/customer benefit?
The goal is too vague and therefore not measurable or verifiable.	**Vague:** Ramp production more quickly. **Measurable:** Ramp up production on Line A as measured by the number of units shipped defect free. **Vague:** Improve teamwork through skip-level meetings. **Verifiable:** Use skip-level meetings to improve teamwork, measured by defined roles and responsibilities with no gaps/overlaps. Further customers do not experience last minute rework owing to product plans not agreed to. Team members are not complaining about each other to the manager but are able to work out differences without manager intervention.	There is no way to tell if this goal has been achieved, or if the progress is being made toward the goal: • What results are you trying to produce? • What is important about the result (how many, how well, cost, when completed)? • What number would you track to evaluate this factor? • What level of performance will be good enough? If you can't measure the goal with a number, describe good performance: • What would you see about the result that means it was done well? • How would you do better if this effort was successful? • What would we hear people saying about the result that means it was produced well? • What would the customer say?

(Continued)

TABLE 3.5 (CONTINUED)

Quick Tips to Improve Goal Setting

Issue/Problem	Examples	How to Improve
The goal is written at the wrong level of the organization (manager vs. subordinate level).	The vice president's (VP's) goal of "Release product to XYZ manufacturing by Q3" should be a business unit's goal. **VP Goal:** Design workflow processes to improve time to market for all new products	These are the goals you would delegate to someone in your organization: • Is this worth measuring at your level? • What unique value do you add? • What is the result you contribute to the effort?
A measured goal is listed but there are no targets.	**Measure only:** Improve high performer turnover rate. **Measure with a specific target:** High performer turnover rate of less than or equal to 5%.	There is a measure for this goal but no specific target to be achieved: • How many, or what percent, do we need to achieve to consider this a success?
The cost (time and resources) of tracking the measures will exceed the value of the data.	A review of the measure of customer satisfaction shows more than 16 possible measures. Creating action items for all of them will likely cost more than what the data are worth.	There are too many measures to track, the measure will be too costly to track, or there is no way to collect the data required. • Will an existing tracking system be "good enough" to use? • Will the value of the data from a new tracking system be worth the cost of collecting the data?

Performance Improvement Plan (PIP)

Through this plan, the organization tries to upgrade itself. The customer and shareholders no longer consider just reaching last year's level of performance acceptable. Expectations arise for an organization, and likewise they must for all employees.

Under APEX, everyone will be focused on continuous performance improvement. All employees should want to work toward achieving their goals. Here, it is recognized that some employees will have more trouble raising their level of performance than others.

Employees are responsible for their performance and performance improvement, with the aid of feedback and coaching from their manager. Each employee is entitled to early, honest, and constructive feedback. By providing this early communication, problems can hopefully be avoided. Prevention is the best course of action.

If an employee does not fully and consistently meet expectations, however, then a manager and an employee will need to engage in corrective action to raise the employee's level of performance. The employee needs to be placed on a PIP and the manager will need to follow the Performance Improvement Process.

Guidelines for PIP

- A PIP is the responsibility of the employee to develop and act upon, with guidance from his or her manager.
- The employee is required to demonstrate immediate and sustained improvement.
- Consequences for unsuccessful completion of a PIP (not immediately improving, or not sustaining improvement) should be specifically identified at the beginning of the PIP and, in nearly all cases, will be termination of employment.
- The typical time frame is 90 days—this gives the employee the opportunity to make the necessary adjustments/improvements, to be sustained. If, however, immediate and sustained improvement is not observed, the PIP can be ended.
- No multiple PIPs. If the employee is not successful, or performance begins to deteriorate again, the employee is not eligible for another PIP.

4

Customer Excellence

The Customer and Market Focus Category examines how your organization determines requirements, expectations, and preferences of customers and markets. Also examined is how your organization builds relationships with customers and determines the key factors that lead to customer acquisition, satisfaction, loyalty and retention, and business expansion and sustainability. Two main questions need to be addressed:

1. How do you identify product offerings to meet the requirements and exceed the expectations of your customer groups through product innovation?
2. How do you identify innovation in product offerings to enter new markets, to attract new customers, and to provide opportunities for expanding relationships with existing customers?

According to our Business System Framework (Table 1.2), this gives rise to the following three processes:

- Value-based pricing and customer value management
- Corporate growth through customer and market knowledge
- Corporate growth through customer relationships and satisfaction

---

VALUE-BASED PRICING AND CUSTOMER VALUE MANAGEMENT

Here is what Sam Walton wrote ...

Sam M. Walton   May 4, 1998
Chairman and Chief Executive Officer

Dear Bob:

I am replying to your letter of the 19th concerning the Wal-Mart monopoly of communities. I have realized for some time and, I suspect, many folks have in the company, as well, how fortunate we are to have very little competition in some of the larger communities in the country. That hasn't always been the case, as you well know. The history of our company has been that we have had more competition early on than most any regional discounter in the United States. However, one by one, our competitors weakened, were mismanaged, and have fallen out in many of the cities. That has been the case generally with Howard's, TG&Y, Gibson, Kuhn's, Magic Mart, and certainly some of the variety chains which were once active in this area. These competitors, plus Alco, Pamida, and the group in Indiana, are on the ropes now and I don't choose to believe those companies disappeared because of our effectiveness. Rather, I choose to believe, for the most part, they were mismanaged and, had they been managed well, there could and would have been enough business in their areas for them and for us....

Value-Based Pricing is a reflection of the value a consumer perceives in the product or service. A consumer's perception of value is based on the consumer's needs, preferences, expectations, financial ability, and what a competitor offers as an alternative.

Concept of Value Creation starts with mission as follows:

> Our mission: "To be our customers' best supplier providing distinctive and highly VALUED products, services and solutions." We understand that we can't create value for our customers if we do not create value for our employees and our investors because the interests of these three groups are inextricably linked.

Business Excellence is based on a belief in how value is created in an organization. Value is created through a cycle of interdependence involving all stakeholders and focused on satisfying customers. All stakeholders have something to contribute and something to gain. The cycle does not function effectively and may even break down if a stakeholder puts in too little or takes out too much.

VALUE CREATION FOR YOUR CUSTOMERS

Your first focus is to create value for your customers. In today's economy, such value creation is based typically on product and process/innovation and on understanding unique customer needs with ever-increasing speed and precision utilizing tools like Quality Function Deployment (QFD), Design for Six Sigma (DFSS), Lean Six Sigma (LSS), Global Quality Management System (GQMS), and Listening and Learning, with methods for customer relationships and customer satisfaction helping create value for customers.

VALUE CREATION FOR YOUR EMPLOYEES

You can innovate and deliver outstanding products only if you tap the commitment, energy, and imagination of your employees. You create value for your employees to motivate and empower them. Value for employees includes being treated respectfully and being involved in decision making. Employees also value meaningful work, competitive compensation opportunities, and continued training and development.

VALUE CREATION FOR YOUR INVESTORS

Creating value for your investors means delivering consistently high returns on their capital. This generally requires both strong revenue growth and attractive profit margins. These, in turn, can be achieved only if a company delivers sustained value for customers.

Setting a price using value-based pricing requires marketing research starting at the product development stage. Market research is carried out to determine how much the typical consumer in your target market values the product or service you are designing as well as particular attributes that are valued the most. You will also need to research and compare your product or service against the products or services offered by the competitors.

Value-based pricing requires a fair degree of advertising to communicate the value of your product or service to your target market. This is especially true if your company is new to the market or you are introducing a new product. The focus of the advertising should be on the attributes of the product or service that provides the greatest perceived value to your target market.

In summary, value-based pricing determines consumers' preferences and desired attributes for a particular product or service and the probable price the customers will pay. Advertising is used to communicate the product attributes that form the basis of the value upon which the price is set.

CORPORATE GROWTH THROUGH CUSTOMER AND MARKET KNOWLEDGE

For a comprehensive understanding of corporate growth through customer and market knowledge and customer relationships and customer satisfaction, the data and methodologies are adopted from several global automotive industries.

LISTENING AND LEARNING METHODS

The core of the customer and market knowledge procedure is the information gathered to support the strategic plan process (Chapter 3) through the Listening and Learning methods presented in Table 4.1. On the basis of this, an industry analysis is conducted, which includes an analysis of market and macroeconomic trends, as well as a review of the company's and competitors' current strategic positioning. The examination of the customer needs encompasses the requirements of potential customers (both new customers and customers with whom the company has previously lost any business) and also the customers of competitive products. Table 4.4 summarizes existing and potential customers and competitors.

On the basis of this analysis, the business segmentation is determined. A five-level segmentation process is adopted (Figure 4.1), which addresses the different and fundamental requirements of the business sector, the region of sale, the channel through which sales are achieved, and the customer type and application of the company's products. The global nature of this business, together with the wide range of products from passenger car to medium

TABLE 4.1

Listening and Learning Methods (Example)

Information Source	OEM	Aftermarket	End User	Dealer	Competitor	Potential Primary Information Sought
Dealer/fleet council		✓	✓	✓		Customer concerns, complaints, future needs
Company corporate planning	✓	✓	✓	✓	✓	Industry and market trends, demographic influences
OEM manufacturers	✓					Impact from legislation, market direction, product changes
Industry functions	✓	✓		✓	✓	Industry trends, personal interaction, performance feedback
Maintenance council (TMC)			✓	✓	✓	Truck groups, field problems, product and performance needs
SAE committee meetings	✓					Product impact from technology, industry recommendations
360° customer reviews	✓	✓			✓	Satisfaction, dissatisfaction, areas for improvement
Call center/Internet	✓	✓	✓		✓	Customer concerns, complaints, competitors' performance
Customer complaints	✓	✓	✓	✓		Areas for improvement
Customer steering committees	✓					Long-term product needs, alignment with new platforms
Dana, autoparts	✓	✓	✓		✓	Regional and global market and customer trends
Research agencies	✓	✓	✓		✓	Market and customer trends, SP data needs
Senior leadership champions	✓	✓	✓			Senior peer-to-peer, business challenges, multilevel feedback

(Continued)

TABLE 4.1 (CONTINUED)

Listening and Learning Methods (Example)

Information Source	OEM	Aftermarket	End User	Dealer	Competitor	Potential Primary Information Sought
Strategic account management association	✓	✓				Objectivity and relevance of account management processes
Surveys	✓	✓	✓	✓	✓	Satisfaction, dissatisfaction, loyalty, comparison to competition
Corporate trends, divisional SP&PP	✓	✓	✓	✓	✓	Corporate strategies and goals
Customer contact/trip reports	✓	✓	✓	✓		Satisfaction, issues, opportunities, competition, customer trends
Road Rangers			✓	✓	✓	Fleet activity, market and dealer needs, product performance
Strategic customer teams	✓	✓				Product performance, opportunities, competitive comparison
Win/loss reports			✓	✓	✓	Analysis of customers choosing competitive product
Regional market plans	✓		✓	✓	✓	Market trends, issues, opportunities, competitive comparison

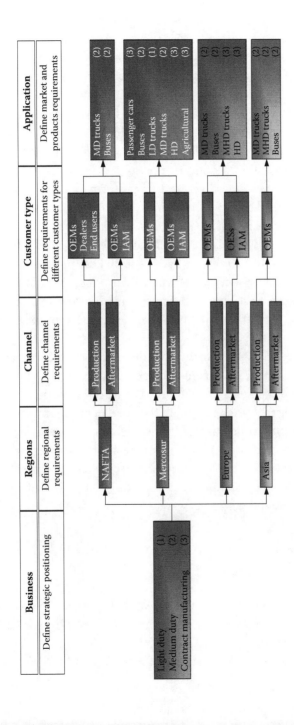

FIGURE 4.1

Example of a five-level company business segmentation for a typical global automotive industry.

and heavy truck, plus the distinctly different commercial environment of contract manufacturing compared with the company's own designed and supported products, mandates this segmentation process. Aligned with the Value Cycle, the segmentation enables different approaches to maximizing Company Value for products from each sector. As an example, the contract manufacturing of gear sets for passenger cars in Mercosur requires focus on high volume and cost-effective manufacturing. Because the company has no intellectual property content in the transmission design of these cars, end-user data and aftermarket issues do not add meaningful value in this sector.

Conversely, the NAFTA Medium Duty market derives significant value from the end-user perception of product performance. Considering the importance of the end users in this region, in 1998, Eaton and Dana signed a marketing agreement. Eaton and Dana products, parts, and support services are marketed as "The Road Ranger System." Products covered include medium and heavy transmissions, clutches, and the MD service tools. The Road Ranger support infrastructure, which includes dedicated field service teams, a 24-hour call center, and Internet web services, is designed to minimize truck downtimes and maximize market exposure for Eaton/Dana products.

Different Listening and Learning methods allow a focused approach within each of the market segment and customer groups.

The market and segments are compared against the business objectives established during the strategic plan. In the event of misalignment between the needs of a segment and business goals, the data are reassessed, further information is sought if required, and where appropriate a new segment is defined. Customers and customer groups are therefore segmented carefully for the business opportunity based on the Company Value provided and the alignment with corporate goals.

INDUSTRY ANALYSIS

An easy way to calculate market growth would be unit and dollar sales for the preceding five years. Without that information, you have to backtrack and gather the historical figures yourself.

Alternatively, there are two methods of gathering this information:

- End-user surveys
- Competitive interviews and analyses

The end-user survey is very expensive because it requires a large sample size. It is also quite time-consuming, particularly when the necessary analysis is required urgently.

The competitive interview and analysis method is preferred. By carefully examining competitor growth rates over a period of years, you can begin to get a firm idea of overall market growth. The accuracy of the method is far from precise, generally within 8% to 10%. However, the information is still extremely informative and perhaps the best you can do cost-effectively.

Even though it is often difficult to get the information from other manufacturers, one can make good use of readily available annual reports, 10-Ks, and quarterly reports, and by interviewing marketing managers, salespeople, and other executives, you can generally put together a pretty good impression of market growth rates.

Unfortunately, when trying to acquire this competitive information, you are going to run into some problems. Virtually nobody in your marketing department or competitive analysis group will want to do it. You will hear some of the following excuses:

"It's unethical. I couldn't do anything like that."
"They will not talk to us. They are the competition."
"I would be embarrassed to make that kind of call."

Remember, nobody will be more surprised than you at how much you can learn from just talking to the competition. Establish your contact with them on an upfront, aboveboard manner and offer to share information with them on an ongoing basis. The benefits of what you learn will far outweigh the costs of what you give away.

To calculate market growth rates accurately, you must weigh each of your competitor's growth rates by its market share. See the example in Table 4.2.

TABLE 4.2

Market Share and Market Growth Measurement

Company	Annual Sales (USD Million)	Market Share (%)	Growth from Previous Year (%)
A	742	48.6	11
B	617	40.4	13
C	105	6.8	24
D	60	3.9	75

MARKET GROWTH RATE AND MARKET SHARE MEASUREMENT

It is essential that a realistic available market size is determined first to assess the profitability of your business.

Table 4.2 shows data collected to determine market share and market growth.

Market growth rate = Change in market size/original market size × 100%

Change in market size = Current market size − original market size

In our example: For Company A, existing market size is 742. At a growth of 11%, the original market size becomes 668.

Table 4.3 summarizes market share growth for companies A, B, C, and D.

Industry analysis gives the company its current positioning in the market. In the example above, the growth arrived at is 14%. Hence, the market share growth = (1333 × 1.14 = ~1520) = 14%. Hence, the strategic plan could lay down a growth of 10% (16.5% or 17%) for the coming year.

CUSTOMER AND MARKET KNOWLEDGE

The core of this procedure is the information gathered to support the strategic plan process through the Listening and Learning methods presented in Table 4.1. The examination of the customer needs encompasses the requirements of potential customers (both new customers and customers with whom you have previously lost any business) and also the customers of competitive products (Table 4.4).

TABLE 4.3

Market Share Growth Measurement

Company	Original Market Size	Current Market Size
A	668	742
B	546	617
C	85	105
D	34	60
Total	1333	1524

TABLE 4.4

Customers and Competitors (Example)

Segments	Customers		Competitor
	Existing	Potentials	
Light trucks	GM, Nissan, Ford, Agrale, DaimlerChrysler, Otokar, VW	DFM, MAN, Iveco, Mitsubishi, Toyota, VW	VI OEM's, ZF (WW—New Venture Gear, Tremec, Aisin Seiki, Getrag)
Medium trucks	International, Iveco, DaimlerChrysler, GM, VW, Ford, Renault (RVI), Volvo, MAN, Paccar, Otokar, BMC, Hino, Isuzu, Mitsubishi, Nissan Diesel, Freightliner, FAW	Otosan, Kamaz, Nivisa, LDV, TATA, Eicher, Bajaj Tempo	VI OEMs, ZF, Allison, TTC
Contract manufacturing	GM	VW, Fiat, Ford, Renault, Peugeot	VI OEMs
• Passenger cars			
• Heavy trucks	Ford, VW (off road), Volvo, International, HD Division	Iveco, VW (on road)	ZF
• Agricultural machines	AGCO (+Valtra), CNH, John-Deere	Yanmar, Agrale, Mahindra&Mahindra	VI OEMs, Pigozzi, ZF
Aftermarket	OEMs, independent distributors	–	Non-genuine parts manufacturers

CUSTOMERS AND COMPETITORS

Table 4.4 summarizes existing and potential customers and competitors.

BUSINESS SEGMENTATION

On the basis of this previous analysis, the business segmentation is determined. A five-level segmentation process is adopted (Figure 4.1), which addresses the different and fundamental requirements of the business sector, the region of sale, the channel through which sales are achieved, and the customer type and application of products.

Example:

Key:

Mercosur: an economic and political agreement among Argentina, Brazil, Paraguay, Uruguay, and Venezuela, with Bolivia becoming an accessing member on December 7, 2012, to be ratified by the Member State's legislatures.

IAM: Independent Aftermarket.

NAFTA: North American Free Trade Agreement.

Listening and Learning methods to determine key customer requirements and expectations, and to identify the key value drivers within each of the business segments, are illustrated in Table 4.1.

Determining the market needs requires a broad knowledge of market sectors and the potential factors that will influence customer purchase decisions not only in the short term but also over the next 5 to 10 years. As such, eliciting accurate customer and market knowledge is a fundamental requirement for the business. This task is championed by the Sales and Marketing Organization. For instance, the long-term goals may highlight the critical requirement for new and highly innovative automated products. These new products allow the creation of significant new customer values and features that will positively differentiate company products from the competition. Defining and assigning values to automated product key features is a complex task. In many areas, progressive companies are innovating ahead of expressed customer product wishes.

General market information is actively pursued through trade organizations, independent consultancies, press articles, and technical symposiums. Macroeconomic trend data highlighting the impact of social, political, and demographic changes can highlight new business opportunities. For instance, the development of the new highway infrastructures in India will have a significant impact on both the truck market volume and the types of trucks demanded by our customers and may offer a new opportunity that is now under investigation.

Emerging new technologies are closely monitored to assess how they could apply to company products or how they could potentially enable competitors to offer higher value solutions. An example of this is the Dual Clutch automation technology recently released in the passenger car market, and how this could affect future medium duty automated products. Pending legislation is also carefully followed, especially for engine gaseous emissions, as this has a significant impact on the future company product requirements and the customer values the company can offer to both vehicle and engine manufacturers.

Company customers are segmented into four main types: the OEMs, Dealers, End Users, and the Independent Aftermarket. The relative importance of these groups varies by region, as illustrated in Figure 4.1. The Listening and Learning channels are tailored to each segment.

PURCHASING FACTORS BY APPLICATION

Segmentation based on the product application is also critical to understand the market and product requirements. Table 4.5 shows some of the typical requirements for different applications.

TABLE 4.5

Purchasing Factors by Application

OEM Segments (Application)	Purchasing Factors			
	Price	**Quality**	**Delivery**	**Service**
Passenger cars	High	High	High	Low
Light trucks	High	High	High	High
Medium trucks	High	High	High	High
Buses	High	High	High	High
Heavy trucks	Medium	Medium	High	High
Agricultural machines	Medium	Medium	High	High

PRICING POLICY

Pricing is a double-edged sword.

"Pricing right" is the fastest way for managers to increase profits. A study of the income statements of 1500 S&P companies by McKinsey consultants revealed that a price rise of 1% would generate an 8% increase in operating profits. This impact is 50% more than that of a 1% fall in variable costs such as materials and direct labor. Also, it is three times greater than the impact of a 1% increase in volume.

But the pricing sword cuts both ways. A decrease of 1% in average prices has the opposite effect, bringing down operating profits by that same 8% if other factors remain steady. Managers may hope that higher volumes will compensate for revenues lost from lower prices and thereby raise profits, but this rarely happens. To continue the examination of typical S&P 1500 economics, volumes would have to rise by 18.7% just to offset the profit impact of a 5% price cut. Such demand sensitivity to price cuts is extremely rare. The moral is: A strategy based on cutting prices to increase volumes and to raise profits is generally doomed to failure in almost every market and industry (McKensey Quarterly November 4, 2015).

THE CUSTOMERS CONSIDER MORE THAN "PRICE" IN DECIDING TO PURCHASE A PRODUCT

Table 4.6 data illustrate that price alone is not the only deciding factor in purchasing a product.

The information gathered through the Listening and Learning processes is communicated via strategic plan and profit plan presentations, divisional quarterly reviews, bimonthly team meetings, customer visit reports, warranty data, monthly reports, and employee communication meetings. On the basis of business value and timing, these customer needs are prioritized and assigned to appropriate teams for implementation. Various methods are used to assist in the filtering and prioritization of new opportunities, including the product planning council, the growth council, and regional growth councils. Throughout this process, the divisional product planning teams work closely with sales and marketing.

For the purposes of product and service planning, the information gained through the methods described is incorporated with DFSS tools

TABLE 4.6

The Customers Consider the Above Factors Above a Set Price

Exhibit 1

Consumers Consider More than Price in Deciding Whether to Purchase a Product

Relevance to Perception of Value for Money	% of Respondents	Description
Price	24	• In general, consistently offers better prices compared with anywhere else • Offers exceptionally low prices from time to time
Experience	17	• I can easily find the specific items I want • This retailer is the most convenient for me to shop
Trust	17	• I know and trust this retailer • The items they sell are always good quality
Assortment	12	• Has good range of prices and quality levels
Return policy	12	• The return policy and process are reasonable and easy to follow
Product research	11	• Retailer makes it easy to find information about items and conduct research
Delivery cost	4	• Has reasonable delivery costs
Loyalty	3	• Has loyalty program that gives me rewards I really value

Source: Q4 2010 McKinsey survey of 6000 U.S. consumers on multichannel pricing and price checks of >1100 items across 20 retailers.

(*The Tactical Guide to Six Sigma Implementation*), including the use of the QFD tool. QFD is used to identify key product attributes and their relative value to customers. As an example, Table 4.7 shows main requirements, identified through QFD, of the second generation of light duty transmission family launched recently.

Table 4.7 is an example of prioritization of customer requirements identified through QFD.

ANALYTICAL HIERARCHY PROCESS

To ensure accurate data, customer surveys are elicited for use in the QFD process above; wherever applicable, use is made of the Analytical Hierarchy Process (AHP). AHP forces a weighted ranking between key product features, as exemplified in Table 4.8.

TABLE 4.7

Requirements Identified through QFD

Comparison[a]	How Much			
	Same	**Somewhat**	**Moderately**	**Extremely**
Assurances				
Base vs. extended warranty	1 2 3	4 5	6 7	8 9
Base vs. durability	1 2 3	4 5	6 7	8 9
Base vs. reliability	1 2 3	4 5	6 7	8 9
Extended vs. durability	1 2 3	4 5	6 7	8 9
Extended vs. reliability	1 2 3	4 5	6 7	8 9
Durability vs. reliability	1 2 3	4 5	6 7	8 9
Functional Performance				
Driver comfort vs. versatility	1 2 3	4 5	6 7	8 9
Driver comfort vs. efficiency	1 2 3	4 5	6 7	8 9
Driver comfort vs. low performance	1 2 3	4 5	6 7	8 9
Versatility vs. efficiency	1 2 3	4 5	6 7	8 9
Versatility vs. low performance	1 2 3	4 5	6 7	8 9
Efficiency vs. low performance	1 2 3	4 5	6 7	8 9
Strategy				
Weight vs. maintainability	1 2 3	4 5	6 7	8 9
Weight vs. resale	1 2 3	4 5	6 7	8 9
Weight vs. operating costs	1 2 3	4 5	6 7	8 9
Maintainability vs. resale	1 2 3	4 5	6 7	8 9
Maintainability vs. operating costs	1 2 3	4 5	6 7	8 9
Resale vs. operating costs	1 2 3	4 5	6 7	8 9
Supply				
Immediate delivery vs. ship premium	1 2 3	4 5	6 7	8 9
Initial Cost				
OEM cost vs. supplier rebate	1 2 3	4 5	6 7	8 9

[a] Circle the more important item on each line.

TABLE 4.8

AHP Example

Requirements	Relative Importance (%)
1. Price	12
2. Quality	20
4. Durability	18
5. Performance	30
9. Selling	10
10. Product finish	10

SELL AND COMMERCIALIZE PRODUCT PROCESS

The day-to-day process of sales and commercialization completes the approach for ensuring the continuing relevance of our products and services and developing new opportunities (Figure 4.2). Throughout this process, customer feedback is carefully monitored to identify potential areas of refinement.

CUSTOMER RELATIONSHIPS AND SATISFACTION

Customer Relationships

The approach to build customer relationship starts with the understanding of customer expectations and needs and includes the definition of the communication channels as described earlier.

A key function in this process is the account manager. Through the sales and marketing organization, account managers are assigned to all current customers. The frequent contacts with key persons build solid relationships and keep both organizations (company and customers) up to date with technical changes, roadmaps, internal reorganizations, corrective actions, and so on, helping to build a solid relationship to satisfy the customers and increase positive referral. See Figure 4.3.

Company additional contact channels (Figure 4.10), which include, besides the account managers and marketing staff, various members of the company management team including product planning, business managers, and general managers as well as several technical functions at the site level, proactively participate in forums or debates on the company business sector and work with their customers' peers for the benefit of their common businesses. Advertisements in trade magazines associating the products with the OEMs are a common practice, but it may be understood that the physical presence is the best approach. One example is the frequent exhibition of a company's current and new products in exhibitions and shows, at which the OEM and aftermarket customers also participate as exhibitors.

Other methods for building relationship include long-term agreements with major OEM customers and a direct contact with dealers, end users, and after sales service staff. The after sales service staff is often asked to test new products. They provide valuable feedback on their performance.

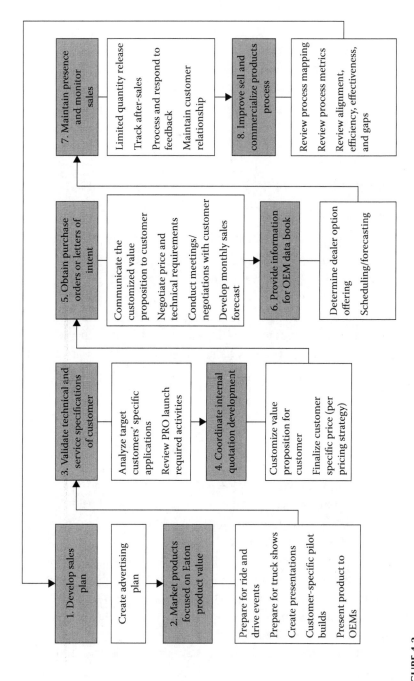

FIGURE 4.2
Sell and commercialize products process.

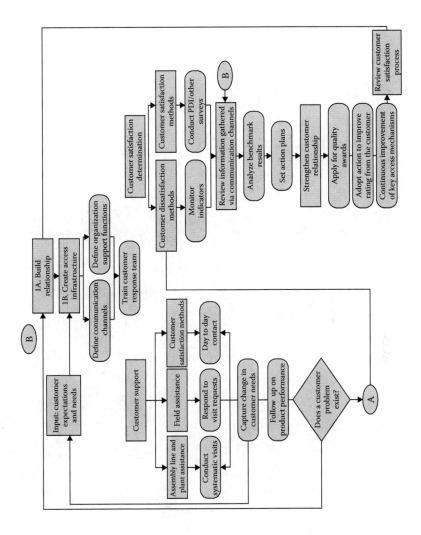

FIGURE 4.3
Manage customer satisfaction process.

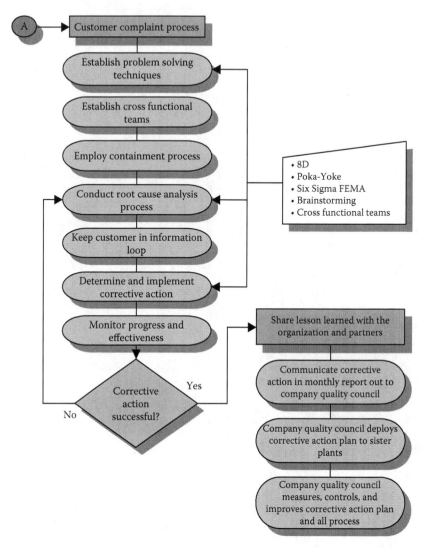

FIGURE 4.4
Customer complaint process.

Partnerships to strengthen the relationship with the customers are identified and established case by case during the strategic plan process.

Manage Customer Satisfaction Process

All of the above practices have demonstrated to be effective in building relationships to acquire and satisfy customers and to increase repeat business and positive referrals, significantly contributing to the company's sales growth.

Customer Access

Table 4.9 shows the main key access mechanisms and technologies used for customers to seek information, conduct business, and make complaints. The main objective of these mechanisms is to provide a clear flow of information and build a strong relationship.

TABLE 4.9

Access Systems

Access Systems	Description
Access technologies	**EDI:** The orders receipt from customers that utilize *electronic data exchange* is safely and efficaciously realized through EDI. In other cases, the communication system includes fax, e-mail, phone, and video or web conference.
	800 Line: Used to facilitate the free access of dealers, sales counters, customer service, truck drivers, and so on. This line can be used to make a suggestion or complaint, clarify technical doubts, and provide support and orientation, as well as to indicate which company representative or repair shop is the closest one to the area the customer is in.
Access functional areas	**Account Managers:** They maintain constant and direct contact with the Original Equipment Manufacturers (OEMs) in their areas. They are an important communication channel between the company and its customers on new products, business opportunities, progress of corrective and preventive actions identified during the customer survey, and the daily contacts (whether in person or by phone).
	Logistic Areas: Customers, who would rather directly contact the factory about their order deliveries than go through the sales team, can also make use of this communication channel. However, the sales team has perfect control over this customer status relative to this aspect.
	Aftermarket Sales Force: Team responsible for receiving aftermarket orders.
	Senior Managers: Visits of senior management at the customer plants.
	Technicians to Call on the Customer Assembly Line: Specific professionals assigned to each customer keep contact with the quality areas of the OEM customers and bring important feedback on company products.
	Field Service Team: Group of professionals specialized in field problem solving.
	Resident Engineers: Depends on the need, the company can hire such professionals to work at the customer's site.
	Product Engineering: Constant contact with customer technical areas ensures alignment with customer needs and products development.

Customer Complaint Process

To ensure that all complaints are resolved effectively and promptly, the company establishes the complaint process presented in Figure 4.4.

The company's mature problem-solving process contributes to the significant improvements of the customer-related metrics. If any of the communication channels receives a customer complaint originating from any of the market segments, a problem-solving team is created. The 8 Disciplines (8D) report is widely used in order to organize the problem resolution (GQMS deals with this extensively). The first step is to identify the containment actions necessary to minimize customer impact pending root cause identification. The company applies a number of different problem-solving techniques, including fundamental tools such as cause-and-effect diagrams and Pareto analysis to more sophisticated practices such as Six Sigma tools. During the whole process, customers are kept informed through the contact channels. After the determination and implementation of corrective actions, the team is responsible for monitoring the effectiveness of the actions of the customer, normally through scheduled visits.

For those more relevant problems, the complaint process is closed only after lesson learned is shared among other company plants. Mechanisms used include monthly reports and the divisional quality council.

Customer Satisfaction Determination

Customer satisfaction and dissatisfaction are determined through the access infrastructure and the following practices:

1. Customer satisfaction survey—This methodology is utilized to assess the degree of satisfaction of all groups of OEM customers and segments. The main objectives of the survey are as follows:
   - To have a systematic process to understand customer satisfaction level
   - Effective use of data delivered, linking with internal performance management process
   - To evaluate competitors' position
   - To predict future performance, using data to drive changes

   It consists of a series of face-to-face interviews with medium and upper management representatives, during which several aspects of company relationship with the customer are evaluated. These interviews are planned according to a predetermined timing chart revised annually and with input from the plants. Typically, the interviewers are company managers in different levels. The interviewee is encouraged to answer questions about future trends, technology, competition, best-in-class suppliers, best practices in the market, new businesses, how the company can improve the relationship, and so on. After the conclusion of all the predetermined interviews, an action plan is designed, indicating the action details, responsible persons, and dates. This action plan is discussed with the involved managers. A summary of the investigated dimensions is given in Table 4.10.

2. Analysis of metrics—A review of customer-related metrics such as product quality at arrival, warranty, and delivery performance provides important pieces of information specially related to eventual customer dissatisfaction. Market share and sales to the top 8 corporate customers are also tracked to monitor growth and customer loyalty.

The combination of these practices with the approaches to Listening and Learning ensures that the measurements capture actionable information that predicts customers' future business with the company and positive referral.

The different approaches utilized to determine satisfaction are kept current with business needs and trends through a continuous learning cycle. The practices to determine customer satisfaction are annually reviewed by the process mapping review and by several other forums such as staff and quality council meetings.

TABLE 4.10

Customer Satisfaction Aspects Assessed by the Customer

Aspect	Questions/Areas
Accessibility	Is it easy to get in touch with the company?
Delivery	Does the company delivery meet the demands?
Facility to negotiate	Is it easy to negotiate with the company?
Quality of product	Does the quality of the company product satisfy your needs?
Quality of attendance	Does the quality of the attendance meet your needs?
Information	Do we provide necessary support information?
Understanding of the needs	Does the company understand your needs?
Competitors	Comparison with competitors performance in all items

5

Operations Focus

The Operations Focus category asks how your organization designs, manages, and improves its products and work processes and improves operational effectiveness to deliver customer value and achieve organizational success and sustainability.

The following two questions are about the excellence requirements that needed to be fulfilled for product and work processes:

1. **Work Processes: How does an organization design, manage, and improve your key products and work processes?**

   Describe how you design, manage, and improve your key work processes to deliver products that achieve customer value and organizational success and sustainability. Summarize your organization's key work processes. In your response, include answers to the following questions:

   a. **Product and Process Design**
      - Design Concepts
        - How do you design your products and work processes to meet all key requirements? How do you incorporate new technology, organizational knowledge, product excellence, and the potential need for agility into these products and processes?
      - Product and Process Requirements
        - How do you determine key product requirements? How do you determine key work process requirements? What are your organization's key work processes? What are the key requirements for these work processes?

b. Process Management
- Process Implementation
  - How does your day-to-day operation of work processes ensure that they meet key process requirements? What key performance measures or indicators and in-process measures do you use to control and improve your work processes? How do these measures relate to end-product quality and performance?
- Support Processes
  - How do you determine your key support processes? What are your key support processes? How does your day-to-day operation of these processes ensure that they meet key business support requirements?
- Product and Process Improvement
  - How do you improve your work processes to improve products and performance and reduce variability?

2. **Operational Effectiveness: How does your organization ensure effective management of its operations on an ongoing basis and for the future?**

Describe how you control costs, manage your supply chain, offer a safe workplace, prepare for potential emergencies, and innovate for the future to ensure effective operations and deliver customer value. In your response, include answers to the following questions:

a. Cost Control

How do you control the overall costs of your operations? How do you incorporate cycle time, productivity, and other efficiency and effectiveness factors into your work processes? How do you prevent defects, service errors, and rework and minimize warranty costs or customers' productivity losses, as appropriate? How do you minimize the costs of inspections, tests, and process or performance audits, as appropriate? How do you balance the need for cost control with the needs of your customers?

b. Supply Chain

How do you manage your supply chain? How do you select suppliers and ensure that they are qualified and positioned to enhance your performance and your customers' satisfaction?

How do you measure and evaluate your suppliers' performance? How do you provide feedback to your suppliers to help them improve? How do you deal with poorly performing suppliers?

c. **Safety and Emergency Preparedness**
   - Safety
     - How do you provide a safe operating environment? How does your safety system address accident prevention, inspection, root-cause analysis of failures, and recovery?
   - Emergency Preparedness
     - How do you ensure that your organization is prepared for disasters or emergencies? How does your disaster and emergency preparedness system consider prevention, continuity of operations, and recovery?

d. **Innovation Management**

How do you manage innovation? How do you pursue the strategic opportunities that you determine are intelligent risks? How do you make the financial and other resources available to pursue these opportunities? How do you discontinue pursuing opportunities at the appropriate time to enhance support for higher-priority opportunities?

Having understood the requirements for excellent operational processes, is it necessary to know from where the inputs to the processes will come? What are the outputs most desired by the stakeholders?

   - Input to process management comes from your short-term (one year) and long-term (five years) strategic planning process.
   - Strategic planning in turn is based on what is important to your stakeholders (customers, employees, equity owners, suppliers, your community) and what are your corporate goals for the current year.

WORK COUNCILS

A better way to fulfill these requirements is through the already established Business Excellence Team assisted by the following four Work Councils:

1. Council for Safety and Culture with a primary goal to implement
   - Philosophy of work practices
   - Management of Environment, Safety, and Health (MESH)
2. Council for Quality (Global Quality Management System [GQMS]) with a primary goal to become
   - The benchmark in quality in your market

3. Council for Speed (Lean Six Sigma [LSS]) with a primary goal to implement
   - LSS
   - Manufacturing cell-based culture
   - Systematic delivery system
4. Council for Cost and Growth (leadership goals) with a primary goal to
   - Drive growth and profitability

In order to qualify for these requirements, most of the Business Excellence models expect that a world-class organization should have effective measures implemented in response to the following questions regarding their work processes, products, and their operational effectiveness:

1. How does your organization determine and prioritize its Key Value Creation and Key Support Processes? How do these processes contribute to the profitability, sustainability, and organizational success?

   What are your organization's Key Value Creation Processes (KVCPs) and Key Support Processes (KSPs)?
2. How does your organization determine its key value creation and key support process requirements?

   What are the key requirements for these processes?
3. How do you design these processes to meet key requirements?

   How do you incorporate new technology?

VALUE CREATION PROCESSES

Value Creation Processes are processes that

- Produce benefit for your customers and for your business.
- Are most important to "running your business."
- Generate your products, your services, and positive business results for your key stakeholders.
- Involve the majority of your employees.

SUPPORT PROCESSES

Support Processes are those that are considered most important for

- Support of your organization's Value Creation Processes.
- Employees.
- Daily operations. These might include facilities management, legal, human resource processes, project management, and administration processes.

Key Value Creation Processes among all organizational processes are prioritized by using a benchmarked **Cause-and-Effect Matrix** (C & E Matrix) tool. This tool is also known as the **Cause-and-Effect Project Prioritization Matrix** when used to prioritize projects or processes on the basis of the quantitative evaluation of their contributions to the creation of value for stakeholders.

C & E MATRIX

C & E Matrix Tool Example

At this stage, it is necessary to become familiar with the C & E Matrix tool.

In the example in Figure 5.1, the hydraulic testing center has 24 testers. It is required to prioritize the three most critical testers to carry out the daily production tests with minimum lost time.

Explanation of C & E Criteria for the example in Figure 5.1:

The hydraulic testing center has 24 testers. The importance of the tester depends on its availability to carry out the tests:

C & E Criteria
9 = Greatest impact
3 = Some impact
1 = Little impact
0 = No impact

The weights are selected on a scale of 1 to 10.

		Criteria							
		10	8	10	10	Wts			
		1	2	3	4				
Item #	Equipment	Back Up Routing Available	Backup Routing Available (outsource)	Overall Volume through Equipment	Current Failures	Total			
1	MDM Tester #1923	9	9	9	9	342			**Criteria**
2	Servo Tester #1909	3	9	9	9	282			Score Demand Hrs
3	Process Water Chiller	9	9	9	1	262			9 > 20
4	160/360 & 1"2"4" Tester #1884	3	9	9	3	222	Tier 1		3 > 10 < 20
5	Reverse Osmosis System	9	3	9	1	214	Critical		1 < 10
6	Gear Motor Tester #819	9	9	1	3	202	Equipment		
7	PVH Tester #8175	1	9	9	3	202			
8	PVH Tester #8112	1	9	9	3	202			Score Backup
9	PVB Tester #1999	1	9	3	9	202			9 No available
10	420 Tester #2011	1	9	3	9	202			3 1 Available
11	Heui Test Stand #8162	9	9	1	1	182			1 More than 1
12	B2B Tester #1838	3	9	3	3	162			
13	Air Compressor	3	3	9	1	154			
14	Gear Pump Tester #1765	1	9	3	3	142			
16	Gear Pump Tester #1474	1	9	3	3	142			Score Fail per week
17	PVE 19/21 Tester #1925	1	9	3	3	142	Tier 2		9 > 3 incidents
18	Triple Test Stand #2031	3	9	1	1	122	Critical		3 1 to 3
19	PVB Tester #8165	1	9	3	1	122	Equipment		1 Less than 1
20	Gear Pump Tester #820	1	9	3	1	122			
21	Lazer Test Stand #1	3	9	1	1	122			
22	Lazer Test Stand #2	3	9	1	1	122			
23	PVH 3 spindle tester #8108	1	9	3	1	122			
24	PVE 12 Tester #2014	1	9	1	1	102			
25						0			
Total		340	384	460	200				

FIGURE 5.1
Cause-and-effect matrix for prioritizing company processes.

Criteria numbers 1, 2, 3, and 4 are explained below:

1. Availability of a backup tester (unavailability of backup makes that tester more important)
   a. Backup not available—Impact 9
   b. Only 1 backup available—Impact 3
   c. More than 1 backup available—Impact 1
2. Availability of an outsourced backup tester (unavailability of backup makes that tester more important)
   a. Backup not available—Impact 9

b. Only 1 backup available—Impact 3

c. More than 1 backup available—Impact 1

3. Demand in hours (more hours means more volume through the equipment)

a. Greater than 20 hours, impact applied—Impact 9

b. Between 10 and 20 hours, impact applied—Impact 3

c. Less than 10 hours, impact applied—Impact 1

4. Number of failures per week (the higher the number of failures, the less the availability for carrying out tests)

a. Number of failures >3—Impact 9

b. Number of failures 1 to 3—Impact 3

c. Number of failures <1—Impact 1

Example: Calculate the score for MDM Tester #1923:

The score = $(9 \times 10) + (9 \times 8) + (9 \times 10) + (9 \times 10) = 342$, and so on.

Rank all testers from high to low.

Prioritization:

It is determined that all testers having a score >200 are designated as Tier 1 Critical Equipment and the rest are designated as Tier 2 Critical Equipment.

Value creation and support processes can be effectively determined by using a **C & E Matrix** tool using the four criteria mentioned above and repeated below:

The importance of the process depends on its contribution to profitability, sustainability, and organizational success.

In order to do this, four criteria are generally recommended by major excellence models.

Criteria 1

Most important to create value for the organization and key stakeholder

Criteria 2

Key to running the business

Criteria 3

Key to achieving positive business results

Criteria 4

Involve the majority of the organization

The following is the process map to answer all three questions posed earlier regarding determination of KVCPs and KSPs.

PROCESS TO DETERMINE KVCPs AND KSPs (FIGURE 5.2)

Step #1

Identify business functions and processes.
   List all actual processes of the organization as an example (Table 5.1).

Step #2

Segregate *value creation* processes from *support* processes by rating the correlation of the processes to the value creation criteria defined in two main questions mentioned at the beginning of this chapter using a C & E Matrix tool.

   The four criteria to be satisfied for ensuring the ongoing effectiveness of the organization that are generally recommended by major excellence models are as follows:

   Criteria 1 (weight 9)
      Most important to create value to organization and key stakeholder
   Criteria 2 (weight 5)
      Key to running your business
   Criteria 3 (weight 7)
      Key to achieving positive business results
   Criteria 4 (weight 8)
      Involve the majority of the organization

   Now, using the C & E Matrix below, assign the impact value of each criterion to each process

   9 = Greatest impact
   3 = Some impact
   1 = Little impact
   0 = No impact

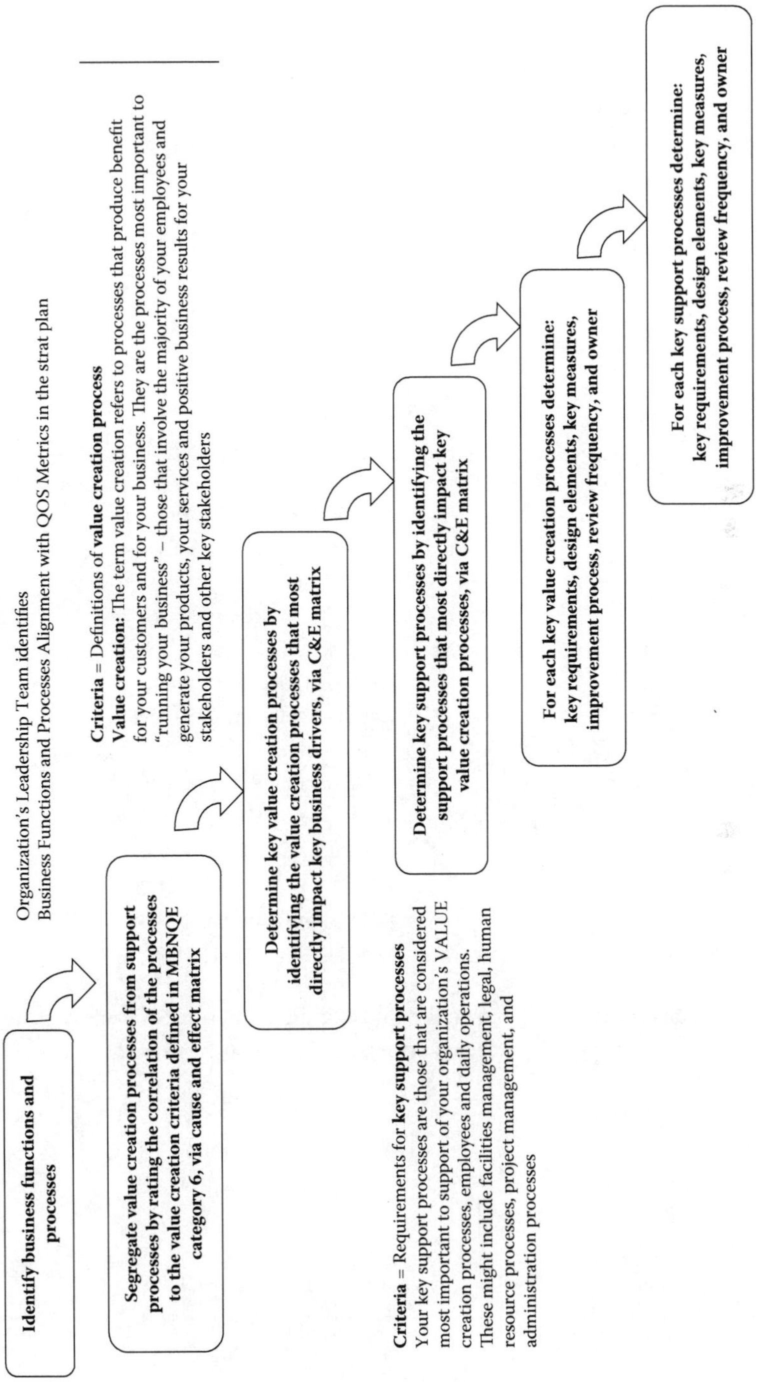

Organization's Leadership Team identifies
Business Functions and Processes Alignment with QOS Metrics in the strat plan

Identify business functions and processes

Segregate value creation processes from support processes by rating the correlation of the processes to the value creation criteria defined in MBNQE category 6, via cause and effect matrix

Criteria = Definitions of **value creation process**
Value creation: The term value creation refers to processes that produce benefit for your customers and for your business. They are the processes most important to "running your business" – those that involve the majority of your employees and generate your products, your services and positive business results for your stakeholders and other key stakeholders

Determine key value creation processes by identifying the value creation processes that most directly impact key business drivers, via C&E matrix

Determine key support processes by identifying the support processes that most directly impact key value creation processes, via C&E matrix

Criteria = Requirements for **key support processes**
Your key support processes are those that are considered most important to support of your organization's VALUE creation processes, employees and daily operations. These might include facilities management, legal, human resource processes, project management, and administration processes

For each key value creation processes determine: key requirements, design elements, key measures, improvement process, review frequency, and owner

For each key support processes determine: key requirements, design elements, key measures, improvement process, review frequency, and owner

FIGURE 5.2
Process to determine key value creation and key support processes.

TABLE 5.1

List of All Processes

Identification of Organization's Business Functions and Processes		
Item	Function	Business Processes
1	Assembly	Assemble valves and manifolds
2	Finance	Cost out
3	Finance	Capital planning
4	Finance	Payroll
5	Finance	Profit planning
6	Finance	Month-end closing
7	Finance	Forecasting
8	Finance	Cost accounting
9	Finance	SOX
10	HR	Performance management
11	HR	Communications
12	HR	Training/employee development
13	HR	Motivation and skills
14	HR	Employee survey
15	HR	EPWP—work systems
16	HR	MESH/ESP
17	HR	Employee suggestion program
18	HR	Round tables/mini-surveys
19	HR	Recruiting
20	HR	Leadership development
21	HR	OCA
22	HR	Community involvement
23	IT	Hardware systems management
24	IT	Software systems management
25	IT	Communications, phone, fax
26	Lean	VSM
27	Maintenance	Equipment, maintenance, and facilities management
28	Manufacturing	Manufacture manifolds, components, and hone cages
29	Manufacturing	Hydraulic test process
30	Materials	Purchasing–SCM
31	LT	Strategic planning
32	Materials	Inventory management
33	Materials	Receiving
34	Materials	Shipping
35	Materials	Supplier viz process, SIOP
36	Materials	Logistics—Import/Export
37	OpEx	Cost out

(Continued)

TABLE 5.1 (CONTINUED)

List of All Processes

	Identification of Organization's Business Functions and Processes	
Item	Function	Business Processes
38	OpEx	Process design (FEMA, WI, PTP)
39	OpEx	PROLaunch
40	OpEx	Plant layout management
41	Quality	Customer quality/RMA/warranty improvement
42	Quality	EQS

Note: OpEx, Operational Excellence.

By using the Excel spreadsheet, the excellence team will get the following total effect values for each process of the organization in this example.

Segregation of KVCPs from support processes through the C & E Matrix is done by drawing a breaking point (the breaking point is where a large gap exists between the next ranking total and where the next ranking total repeats significantly). In the matrix in Table 5.2, a breaking point is below the strategic planning process after which the large gap is seen at the GQMS process.

Through the C & E Matrix in Table 5.2, we have identified the following KVCPs and their functions as shown in Table 5.3.

Step #3

Determine KVCPs by identifying the value creation processes that most directly affect key business drivers, via the C & E Matrix.

Having identified the VCPs, we need to find out how each VCP affects Key Business Drivers (KBDs). **The idea is to select few vital VCPs (KVCPs) that greatly contribute to organizational effectiveness.**

The KBDs are as follows:

- Safety
  - The KBD metrics being
    - MESH deployment
    - Recordable injury rate
- Quality
  - The KBD metrics being
    - ISO/TS/GQMS
    - Customer DPPM

TABLE 5.2

Segregation of Value Creation Processes from Support Processes

| | | | | Criteria 1 | Criteria 2 | Criteria 3 | Criteria 4 | Weight |
| Rank | Type | Function | Process | 9 | 5 | 7 | 8 | |
				Most Important to Create Value to Organization and Key Stakeholder	Key to Running Your Business	Key to Achieving Positive Business Results	Involve the Majority of the Organization	Total
1	VC	Assembly	Assemble SICVs and MCDs	9	9	9	9	2610
1	VC	Mfg	Manufacture manifolds, components, and hone cages	9	9	9	9	2610
3	VC	Quality	Customer quality/RMA/warranty improvement	9	3	9	9	2310
4	VC	SCM	Cost out	9	9	3	9	2190
5	VC	Materials	Purchasing–SCM	9	9	9	3	2130
5	VC	SLT	Strategic planning	9	9	9	3	2130
7	SP	Quality	GQMS	3	3	9	9	1770
8	SP	Lean	VSM	3	9	9	3	1590
8	SP	Mfg	Hydraulic test process	3	9	9	3	1590
10	SP	HR	Performance management	0	1	9	9	1400
11	SP	HR	Communications	0	9	3	9	1380
11	SP	HR	Training/employee development	0	9	3	9	1380
13	SP	Materials	Inventory management	0	9	9	3	1320

(Continued)

TABLE 5.2 (CONTINUED)

Segregation of Value Creation Processes from Support Processes

| | | | | Criteria 1 | Criteria 2 | Criteria 3 | Criteria 4 | Weight ⬇ |
| | | | | 9 | 5 | 7 | 8 | |
Rank	Type	Function	Process	Most Important to Create Value to Organization and Key Stakeholder	Key to Running Your Business	Key to Achieving Positive Business Results	Involve the Majority of the Organization	Total
14	SP	OpEx	Process design (FEMA, WI, PTP)	3	3	1	9	1210
15	SP	HR	Employee survey	0	3	3	9	1080
15	SP	HR	EPWP—work systems	0	3	3	9	1080
15	SP	HR	MESH/ESP	0	3	3	9	1080
15	SP	HR	Employee suggestion program	0	3	3	9	1080
19	SP	HR	Round tables/mini-surveys	0	1	3	9	980
20	SP	HR	Recruiting	0	9	3	3	900
20	SP	HR	Leadership development	0	9	3	3	900
20	SP	Finance	Capital planning	0	9	3	3	900
23	SP	Finance	Payroll	0	9	3	1	740
24	SP	OpEx	PROLaunch	3	3	3	1	710
25	SP	HR	OCA	0	3	3	3	600

(Continued)

Segregation of Value Creation Processes from Support Processes

Cause-and-Effect Matrix

TABLE 5.2 (CONTINUED)

Segregation of Value Creation Processes from Support Processes

Rank	Type	Function	Process	Criteria 1 9 Most Important to Create Value to Organization and Key Stakeholder	Criteria 2 5 Key to Running Your Business	Criteria 3 7 Key to Achieving Positive Business Results	Criteria 4 8 Involve the Majority of the Organization	Weight ⬇ Total
				Segregation of Value Creation Processes from Support Processes Cause-and-Effect Matrix				
25	SP	Materials	Receiving	0	3	3	3	600
25	SP	Materials	Shipping	0	3	3	3	600
25	SP	Finance	Profit planning	0	9	1	1	600
29	SP	IT	Hardware systems management	1	3	3	1	530
29	SP	IT	Software systems management	1	3	3	1	530
29	SP	IT	Communications, phone, fax	1	3	3	1	530
29	SP	Maintenance	Equipment, maintenance, and facilities management	1	3	3	1	530
33	SP	Materials	Supplier viz process, SIOP	0	3	3	1	440
34	SP	HR	Community involvement	0	1	1	3	360
35	SP	Finance	Month-end closing	0	3	1	1	300
35	SP	Finance	Forecasting	0	3	1	1	300

(Continued)

TABLE 5.2 (CONTINUED)

Segregation of Value Creation Processes from Support Processes

				Criteria 1 9 Most Important to Create Value to Organization and Key Stakeholder	Criteria 2 5 Key to Running Your Business	Criteria 3 7 Key to Achieving Positive Business Results	Criteria 4 8 Involve the Majority of the Organization	Weight ⬇
Rank	**Type**	**Function**	**Process**					**Total**
35	SP	Finance	Cost accounting	0	3	1	1	300
35	SP	Materials	Logistics—import/export	0	3	1	1	300
39	SP	Finance	SOX	0	3	0	1	230

Instructions

1. Enter Value Creation Process Definitions from Criteria Section 6.1(a)
2. Enter Plant Functions and Processes
3. Rate Impact of Process on Creating Value (defined above) for Organization, Customers, and Other Key Stakeholders per Criteria
4. Rank Totals (high to low) and Identify Top Ranking Processes That Correlate Most to Creating Value by Drawing a Breaking Point (the breaking point is where a large gap exists between the next ranking total and where the next ranking total repeats significantly)
5. Top Ranking Processes Are Deemed "Value Creation Processes"; Others Are Considered "Support Processes"

Criteria

9 = Greatest impact
3 = Some impact
1 = Little impact
0 = No impact

Example: Assembly Process Impact = $(9 \times 9 + 9 \times 5 + 9 \times 7 + 9 \times 8)10 = 2610$, and so on.

Note: Impact value of 261 is amplified by multiplying by 10.

Weights

On a scale of 1 to 10

TABLE 5.3

Selection of Key Value Creation Processes

Function	Process
Assembly	Assemble SICVs and MCDs
Mfg	Manufacture manifolds, components, and hone cages
Quality	Customer quality/RMA/warranty improvement
SCM	Cost out
Materials	Purchasing–SCM
Strat Leadership Team (SLT)	Strategic planning

- Supplier DPPM
- RTY
- Test FPY
- Speed
  - The KBD metrics being
    - Supplier on-time delivery (OTD)
    - Days on hand (DOH)
    - Customer OTD
- Cost
  - The KBD metrics being
    - Scrap
    - Cost of nonconformance (CONC)
    - Cost out materials (materials cost reduction)
    - Cost out Lean (cost reduction due to Lean implementation)
    - Incremental/decremental (**incremental** costs refer to an increase in cost between two alternatives—one alternative to another; decrease in cost should be referred to as **decremental** cost)
- Involvement of majority of the organization

Now, we need to rate the impact of each one of these VCPs on each KBD metric.

Referring to the spreadsheet (Table 5.4), we can see that the totals are ranked from high to low and the top-ranking VCPs that most greatly affect key business metrics are identified by drawing a breaking point (the breaking point is where a large gap exists between the next ranking total and where the next ranking total repeats significantly).

TABLE 5.4

Prioritization of Key Value Creation Processes

Determination of Key Value Creation Processes

Weight ⬇

Rank	Type	Function	Value Creation Processes	Safety (10)		Quality (10)						Speed (10)			Cost (10)					Involve the Majority of the Organization (10)	Key Business Drivers Total
				MESH	Injury Rate	ISO/TS	CUST DPPM	SUPP DPPM	RTY	TEST FPY	SUPP OTD	DOH	CUST OTD	SCRAP	CONC	COST OUT MAT	COST OUT LEAN	INC/DEC		
1	KVC	Assembly	Assemble valves	3	9	9	9	9	9	9	9	9	9	9	9	9	9	9	9	1380
1	KVC	Manufacturing	Machine manifolds, hone cages	3	9	9	9	9	9	9	9	9	9	9	9	9	9	9	9	1380
3	KVC	SCM	Cost out	0	0	3	9	3	3	9	3	9	3	9	9	9	9	9	9	960
3	KVC	RLT	Strategic planning	0	0	3	9	3	3	3	9	9	9	3	3	9	3	9	3	960
5		Quality	Customer DPPM, RMA	0	0	3	9	9	9	9	0	3	3	0	0	0	0	0	9	540
5		Materials	Purchasing	0	0	3	3	3	3	3	9	3	0	0	0	9	0	3	9	540

Key Business Drivers

Instructions

1. Enter Value Creation Process Definitions from Criteria Section 6.1(a)
2. Enter Plant Functions and Processes
3. Rate Impact of Process on Creating Value (defined above) for Organization, Customers, and Other Key Stakeholders per Criteria
4. Rank Totals (high to low) and Identify Top Ranking Processes That Correlate Most to Creating Value by Drawing a Breaking Point (the breaking point is where a large gap exists between the next ranking total and where the next ranking total repeats significantly)
5. Top Ranking Processes Are Deemed "Value Creation Processes"; Others Are Considered "Support Processes"

Criteria

9 = Greatest impact
3 = Some impact
1 = Little impact
0 = No impact
Weights on a scale of 1 to 10

In summary, we have the following KVCPs that affect organizational effectiveness to the greatest extent.

		Function	Value Creation Process
1	KVC	Assembly	Assemble SICVs and MCDs
1	KVC	Manufacturing	Manufacture manifolds, components, and hone cages
3	KVC	SCM	Cost out
3	KVC	RLT	Strategic planning

Step #4

Determine key support processes by identifying the support processes that most directly affect KVCPs, via the C & E Matrix.

KSPs support your organization's VALUE CREATION processes, employees, and daily operations.

Support processes affect KVCPs to promote

- Safety
- Quality
- Customer satisfaction
- Profitability

For each Value Creation Process, we will use the C & E Matrix to prioritize the support processes.

For example, in the case of **Assembly (VCP)**, out of all the support processes of the organization, the **"Purchasing" support process** affects this VCP to the greatest extent as shown in the C & E Matrix in Table 5.5. The impact points are calculated as follows:

For safety, 30 (10×3) impact points
For quality, 72 (9×8) impact points
For customer satisfaction, 63 (9×7) impact points
For profitability, 63 (9×7) impact points
- Purchasing Support Process has 228 impact points.
- Test Process has 228 impact points.
- HR has 204 impact points.

TABLE 5.5

Determination of Key Support Processes for KVC Process Assembly

Determination of Key Support Processes Cause-and-Effect Matrix

Key Value Creation Process

| | | | | Weight → | 1 (10) | 2 (8) | 3 (7) | 4 (7) | |
| | | | | | | Assembly | | | |
Function	Support Processes	Rank	Type		Safety	Quality	Customer Satisfaction	Profitability	Total
Materials	Purchasing–SCM	1	KSP		3	9	9	9	228
HR	Training/employee development	3	KSP		9	9	3	3	204
Manufacturing	Hydraulic test process	1	KSP		3	9	9	9	228
Quality	Customer quality/RMA/warranty improvement	4			1	9	9	3	166
Lean	VSM	5			1	3	9	9	160
HR	MESH/ESP	6			9	3	3	1	142
OpEx	Process design (FEMA, WI, PTP)	7			3	9	3	1	130
Finance	Profit planning	8			1	1	3	9	102
HR	Performance management	9			3	3	3	3	96
HR	Communications	9			3	3	3	3	96
HR	EPWP—work systems	9			3	3	3	3	96
HR	Leadership development	9			3	3	3	3	96
Maintenance	Equipment, maintenance, and facilities management	9			3	3	3	3	96
Finance	Month-end closing	14			1	1	1	9	88
Finance	Cost accounting	14			1	1	1	9	88

(Continued)

TABLE 5.5 (CONTINUED)

Determination of Key Support Processes for KVC Process Assembly

	Determination of Key Support Processes Cause-and-Effect Matrix			Weight	1	2	3	4	
				⌐→	10	8	7	7	
							Assembly		
							Customer		
	Key Value Creation Process								
Function	Support Processes	Rank	Type	Safety	Quality	Satisfaction	Profitability	Total
HR	Employee survey	14		1	1	9	1	88
HR	Round tables/mini-surveys	14		1	1	9	1	88
Materials	Supplier viz process, SIOP	18		0	0	9	3	84
Finance	Capital planning	23		1	3	1	3	62
IT	Software systems management	19		1	3	3	3	76
IT	Communications, phone, fax	19		1	3	3	3	76
Materials	Inventory management	19		1	3	3	3	76
OpEx	PROLaunch	19		1	3	3	3	76
HR	Recruiting	23		1	3	3	3	62
Quality	EQS	23		1	3	3	1	62
IT	Hardware systems management	26		1	1	3	3	60
Finance	Payroll	27		1	1	1	3	46
Finance	Forecasting	27		1	1	1	3	46
Finance	SOX	27		1	1	3	1	46
HR	Employee suggestion program	27		1	1	1	3	46
HR	OCA	27		1	1	1	3	46

(Continued)

TABLE 5.5 (CONTINUED)

Determination of Key Support Processes for KVC Process Assembly

Determination of Key Support Processes Cause-and-Effect Matrix

		Weight ⤷	1	2	3	4	
			10	8	7	7	
					Assembly		

Key Value Creation Process

| | | | | | | Customer | | |
Function	Support Processes	Rank	Type	Safety	Quality	Satisfaction	Profitability	Total
Materials	Receiving	27		1	1	3	1	46
Materials	Shipping	27		1	1	3	1	46
Materials	Logistics—import/export	27		1	1	3	1	46
HR	Community involvement	35		1	1	1	1	32

Instructions

1. Enter Key Value Creation Processes (from Key Value Creation C & E Matrix)
2. Enter Support Processes (from Value Creation and Support C & E Matrix)
3. Rate Importance of Support Process on Key Value Creation Process per Criteria
4. Rank Totals (high to low) and Identify Top Ranking Support Processes That Most Greatly Affect Value Creation Processes by Drawing a Breaking Point (the breaking point is where a large gap exists between the next ranking total and where the next ranking total repeats significantly)
5. Support Processes That Most Greatly Affect Value Creation Processes Are Deemed "Key Support Processes"

Criteria

How Does Support Process Affect Value Creation Processes?

9 = Greatest impact
3 = Some impact
1 = Little impact
0 = No impact

Weights

On a scale of 1 to 10

Assembly (Key Value Creation Process)

In summary, we have the following KSPs that support KVCP assembly.

		Function	Key Support Process
1	KSP	Purchasing–SCM	Purchasing
2	KSP	Training	Employee development
3	KSP	Test	Customer requirement compliance

Manufacturing (Key Value Creation Process)

Here, Purchasing–SCM (Supply Chain Management) and HR support processes affect manufacturing to the greatest extent as shown in Table 5.6.

In summary, we have the following KSPs that support KVCP manufacturing.

Materials	Purchasing–SCM	KSP
HR	Training/employee development	KSP

Cost Out (Key Value Creation Process)

This process is also affected greatly by Purchasing and HR support processes as seen in the C & E Matrix in Table 5.7.

In summary, we have the following KSP that supports KVCP cost out.

Materials	Purchasing–SCM	1	KSP
HR	Training/employee development	2	KSP

Strategic Planning (Key Value Creation Process)

This process is also greatly affected by Purchasing and HR support processes as seen in the C & E Matrix in Table 5.8.

In summary, we have the following KSP that supports KVCP strategic planning.

Materials	Purchasing–SCM	1	KSP
HR	Training/employee development	2	KSP

Now, we have the following common KSPs supporting the KVCPs shown in Table 5.9.

TABLE 5.6

Determination of Key Support Processes for KVC Process Manufacturing

Determination of Key Support Processes Cause-and-Effect Matrix				Weight ⤴			Manufacturing		
				5	6	7		8	
				10	8	7		7	
Key Value Creation Process							Customer		
Function	Support Processes	Rank	Type	Safety	Quality	Satisfaction	Profitability		Total
Materials	Purchasing–SCM	2	KSP	3	9	9	9		228
HR	Training/employee development	1	KSP	9	9	3	9		246
Manufacturing	Hydraulic test process	9		3	3	3	3		96
Quality	Customer quality/RMA/warranty Improvement	3		1	9	9	3		166
Lean	VSM	4		1	3	9	9		160
HR	MESH/ESP	5		9	3	3	1		142
OpEx	Process design (FEMA, WI, PTP)	6		3	9	3	1		130
Finance	Profit planning	8		1	1	3	9		102
HR	Performance management	9		3	3	3	3		96
HR	Communications	9		3	3	3	3		96
HR	EPWP—work systems	9		3	3	3	3		96
HR	Leadership development	9		3	3	3	3		96
Maintenance	Equipment, maintenance, and facilities management	9		3	3	3	3		96
Finance	Month-end closing	15		1	1	1	9		88
Finance	Cost accounting	15		1	1	1	9		88

(*Continued*)

TABLE 5.6 (CONTINUED)

Determination of Key Support Processes for KVC Process Manufacturing

Determination of Key Support Processes Cause-and-Effect Matrix

Key Value Creation Process

				Weight				
				⬆		Manufacturing		
				5	6	7	8	
				10	**8**	**7**	**8**	
						Customer		
Function	**Support Processes**	**Rank**	**Type**	**Safety**	**Quality**	**Satisfaction**	**Profitability**	**Total**
HR	Employee survey	15		1	1	9	1	88
HR	Round tables/mini-surveys	15		1	1	9	1	88
Materials	Supplier viz process, SIOP	19		0	0	9	3	84
Finance	Capital planning	7		1	3	1	9	104
IT	Software systems management	20		1	3	3	3	76
IT	Communications, phone, fax	20		1	3	3	3	76
Materials	Inventory management	20		1	3	3	3	76
OpEx	PROLaunch	20		1	3	3	3	76
HR	Recruiting	24		1	3	1	3	62
Quality	EQS	24		1	3	3	1	62
IT	Hardware systems management	26		1	1	3	3	60
Finance	Payroll	27		1	1	1	3	46
Finance	Forecasting	27		1	1	1	3	46
Finance	SOX	27		1	1	3	1	46
HR	Employee suggestion program	27		1	1	1	3	46
HR	OCA	27		1	1	1	3	46

(Continued)

TABLE 5.6 (CONTINUED)

Determination of Key Support Processes for KVC Process Manufacturing

Determination of Key Support Processes Cause-and-Effect Matrix

				5	6	7	8	
	Weight ⤵			10	8	7	7	
						Manufacturing		
Key Value Creation Process						Customer		
Function	Support Processes	Rank	Type	Safety	Quality	Satisfaction	Profitability	Total
Materials	Receiving	27		1	1	3	1	46
Materials	Shipping	27		1	1	3	1	46
Materials	Logistics—import/export	27		1	1	3	1	46
HR	Community involvement	35		1	1	1	1	32

Instructions

1. Enter Key Value Creation Processes (from Key Value Creation C & E Matrix)
2. Enter Support Processes (from Value Creation and Support C & E Matrix)
3. Rate Importance of Support Process on Key Value Creation Process per Criteria
4. Rank Totals (high to low) and Identify Top Ranking Support Processes That Most Greatly Affect Value Creation Processes by Drawing a Breaking Point (the breaking point is where a large gap exists between the next ranking total and where the next ranking total repeats significantly)
5. Support Processes That Most Greatly Affect Value Creation Processes Are Deemed "Key Support Processes"

Criteria

How Does Support Process Affect Value Creation Processes?

9 = Greatest impact
3 = Some impact
1 = Little impact
0 = No impact

Weights

On a scale of 1 to 10

TABLE 5.7

Prioritization of How Key Support Processes Affect Value Creation Process for KVC Process Cost Out

Determination of Key Support Processes Cause-and-Effect Matrix				Weight		Cost Out		
				10	8	7	7	
				9	10	11	12	
Key Value Creation Process						Customer		
Function	Support Processes	Rank	Type	Safety	Quality	Satisfaction	Profitability	Total
Materials	Purchasing–SCM	1	KSP	3	9	9	9	228
HR	Training/employee development	2	KSP	0	9	9	3	156
Manufacturing	Hydraulic test process	34		1	1	1	1	32
Quality	Customer quality/RMA/warranty improvement	3		1	9	9	1	152
Lean	VSM	5		3	3	3	3	96
HR	MESH/ESP	18		3	3	3	1	82
OpEx	Process design (FEMA, WI, PTP)	4		3	9	3	1	130
Finance	Profit planning	11		1	1	1	9	88
HR	Performance management	5		3	3	3	3	96
HR	Communications	5		3	3	3	3	96
HR	EPWP—work systems	5		3	3	3	3	96
HR	Leadership development	5		3	3	3	3	96
Maintenance	Equipment, maintenance, and facilities management	5		3	3	3	3	96
Finance	Month-end closing	11		1	1	1	9	88
Finance	Cost accounting	11		1	1	1	9	88

(Continued)

TABLE 5.7 (CONTINUED)

Prioritization of How Key Support Processes Affect Value Creation Process for KVC Process Cost Out

Determination of Key Support Processes Cause-and-Effect Matrix		Weight ⤷		9	10	11	12
				10	8	7	7
Key Value Creation Process						Cost Out	
						Customer	
Function	Support Processes	Rank	Type	Safety	Quality	Satisfaction	Profitability	Total
HR	Employee survey	11		1	1	9	1	88
HR	Round tables/mini-surveys	11		1	1	9	1	88
Materials	Supplier viz process, SIOP	17		0	0	9	3	84
Finance	Capital planning	23		1	3	1	3	62
IT	Software systems management	19		1	3	3	3	76
IT	Communications, phone, fax	19		1	3	3	3	76
Materials	Inventory management	19		1	3	3	3	76
OpEx	PROLaunch	19		1	3	3	3	76
HR	Recruiting	23		1	3	1	3	62
Quality	EQS	23		1	3	3	1	62
IT	Hardware systems management	26		1	1	3	3	60
Finance	Payroll	27		1	1	1	3	46
Finance	Forecasting	27		1	1	1	3	46
Finance	SOX	27		1	1	3	1	46
HR	Employee suggestion program	11		1	1	1	9	88
HR	OCA	27		1	1	1	3	46

(Continued)

TABLE 5.7 (CONTINUED)

Prioritization of How Key Support Processes Affect Value Creation Process for KVC Process Cost Out

Determination of Key Support Processes Cause-and-Effect Matrix

						Cost Out		
Weight ⤷				9	10	11	12	
				10	8	7	7	
Key Value Creation Process						**Customer**		
Function	Support Processes	Rank	Type	Safety	Quality	Satisfaction	Profitability	Total
Materials	Receiving	27		1	1	3	1	46
Materials	Shipping	27		1	1	3	1	46
Materials	Logistics—import/export	27		1	1	3	1	46
HR	Community Involvement	34		1	1	1	1	32

Instructions

1. Enter Key Value Creation Processes (from Key Value Creation C & E Matrix)
2. Enter Support Processes (from Value Creation and Support C & E Matrix)
3. Rate Importance of Support Process on Key Value Creation Process per Criteria
4. Rank Totals (high to low) and Identify Top Ranking Support Processes That Most Greatly Affect Value Creation Processes by Drawing a Breaking Point (the breaking point is where a large gap exists between the next ranking total and where the next ranking total repeats significantly)
5. Support Processes That Most Greatly Affect Value Creation Processes Are Deemed "Key Support Processes"

Criteria

How Does Support Process Affect Value Creation Processes?

9 = Greatest impact
3 = Some impact
1 = Little impact
0 = No impact

Weights

On a scale of 1 to 10

TABLE 5.8

Prioritization of How Key Support Processes Affect Value Creation Process for KVC Process Strategic Planning

Determination of Key Support Processes Cause-and-Effect Matrix		Weight ⤷		13	14	15	16	
				10	8	7	7	
					Strat Planning			
Key Value Creation Process						Customer		
Function	Support Processes	Rank	Type	Safety	Quality	Satisfaction	Profitability	Total
Materials	Purchasing–SCM	1	KSP	9	9	9	9	288
HR	Training/employee development	2	KSP	0	9	9	3	156
Manufacturing	Hydraulic test process	34		1	1	1	1	32
Quality	Customer quality/RMA/warranty improvement	18		1	3	3	3	76
Lean	VSM	5		3	3	3	3	96
HR	MESH/ESP	17		3	3	3	1	82
OpEx	Process design (FEMA, WI, PTP)	3		3	9	3	1	130
Finance	Profit planning	11		1	1	1	9	88
HR	Performance management	5		3	3	3	3	96
HR	Communications	5		3	3	3	3	96
HR	EPWP—work systems	5		3	3	3	3	96
HR	Leadership development	5		3	3	3	3	96
Maintenance	Equipment, maintenance, and facilities management	5		3	3	3	3	96
Finance	Month-end closing	11		1	1	1	9	88

(Continued)

TABLE 5.8 (CONTINUED)

Prioritization of How Key Support Processes Affect Value Creation Process for KVC Process Strategic Planning

Determination of Key Support Processes Cause-and-Effect Matrix		Weight		13	14	15	16	
		⬆		10	8	7	7	
						Strat Planning		
Key Value Creation Process								
						Customer		
Function	Support Processes	Rank	Type	Safety	Quality	Satisfaction	Profitability	Total
Finance	Cost accounting	11		1	1	1	9	88
HR	Employee survey	11		1	1	9	1	88
HR	Round tables/mini-surveys	11		1	1	9	1	88
Materials	Supplier viz process, SIOP	16		0	0	9	3	84
Finance	Capital planning	23		1	3	1	3	62
IT	Software systems management	18		1	3	3	3	76
IT	Communications, phone, fax	18		1	3	3	3	76
Materials	Inventory management	18		1	3	3	3	76
OpEx	PROLaunch	18		1	3	3	3	76
HR	Recruiting	23		1	3	1	3	62
Quality	EQS	23		1	3	3	1	62
IT	Hardware systems management	26		1	1	3	3	60
Finance	Payroll	27		1	1	1	3	46
Finance	Forecasting	27		1	1	1	3	46
Finance	SOX	27		1	1	3	1	46
HR	Employee suggestion program	27		1	1	1	3	46

(Continued)

TABLE 5.8 (CONTINUED)

Prioritization of How Key Support Processes Affect Value Creation Process for KVC Process Strategic Planning

Determination of Key Support Processes Cause-and-Effect Matrix

		Weight →		13	14	15	16	
				10	8	7	7	
					Strat Planning			
						Customer		
Function	Support Processes	Rank	Type	Safety	Quality	Satisfaction	Profitability	Total
HR	OCA	4		1	9	1	3	110
Materials	Receiving	27		1	1	3	1	46
Materials	Shipping	27		1	1	3	1	46
Materials	Logistics—import/export	27		1	1	3	1	46
HR	Community involvement	34		1	1	1	1	32

Key Value Creation Process

Instructions

1. **Enter Key Value Creation Processes** (from Key Value Creation C & E Matrix)

2. **Enter Support Processes** (from Value Creation and Support C & E Matrix)

3. **Rate Importance of Support Process on Key Value Creation Process per Criteria**

4. **Rank Totals** (high to low) **and Identify Top Ranking Support Processes That Most Greatly Affect Value Creation Processes by Drawing a Breaking Point** (the breaking point is where a large gap exists between the next ranking total and where the next ranking total repeats significantly)

5. **Support Processes That Most Greatly Affect Value Creation Processes Are Deemed "Key Support Processes"**

Criteria

How Does Support Process Affect Value Creation Processes?

9 = **Greatest impact**

3 = **Some impact**

1 = **Little impact**

0 = **No impact**

Weights

On a scale of 1 to 10

TABLE 5.9

Determination of Key Support Processes

	Function	Key Support Process
KSP	SCM	Purchasing–SCM
KSP	HR	Training/employee development
KSP	Test engineering	Hydraulic test process

Step #5

For each KVCP, determine key requirements, design elements, key measures, improvement process, review frequency, and owner.

The Product and Process Requirements for each VCP are determined by answering the following questions:

- How do you determine key product requirements?
- How do you design key work process elements?
- What are key process measures?
- How do you minimize costs?
- What are the improvement processes?
- How often are these processes reviewed?
- Who is the owner of these processes?

Table 5.10 summarizes how these requirements are met.

Step #6

For each KSP, determine key requirements, design elements, key measures, improvement process, review frequency, and owner.

The Product and Process Requirements for each KSP are determined by answering the following questions:

- How do you determine key product requirements?
- How do you design key work process elements?
- What are key process measures?
- How do you minimize costs?
- What are the improvement processes?
- How often are these processes reviewed?
- Who is the owner of these processes?

Table 5.11 summarizes how these requirements are met.

TABLE 5.10

Determine Product and Process Requirements for Each Key Value Creation Process

Value Creation Processes	Key Requirements	Design Elements	Key Measures	Minimization of Costs	Improvement Process	Review Frequency	Owner
Assembly Assemble valves and manifolds	Safety Quality Profitability Customer satisfaction	LSS tools PROLaunch GQMS Process ownership	Recordable injury rate Customer DPPM OTD LSS score GQMS score PROLaunch score RTY RMA response time	GQMS 7 product realization policies and 8 measurement analysis and improvement policies book 1	QOS plant and floor level Value stream map Customer focus MESH focus Employee survey Benchmark 8D process	Weekly QOS Monthly QOS All product realization processes reviewed twice a year	Assembly supervisor
Manufacturing Manufacture manifolds, components, and hone cages	Safety Quality Profitability Customer satisfaction	LSS tools PROLaunch GQMS Process ownership CNC programming	Recordable injury rate OTD LSS score GQMS score PROLaunch score RTY	GQMS 7 product realization policies and 8 measurement analysis and improvement policies	QOS plant and floor level Value stream map Customer focus MESH focus Employee survey Benchmark 8D process	Weekly QOS Monthly QOS All product realization processes reviewed twice a year	Plant manager

(Continued)

TABLE 5.10 (CONTINUED)

Determine Product and Process Requirements for Each Key Value Creation Process

Value Creation Processes	Key Requirements	Design Elements	Key Measures	Minimization of Costs	Improvement Process	Review Frequency	Owner
Cost Out	Safety Quality Profitability Customer satisfaction	PROLaunch GQMS LSS Sourcing process progress tracker	Cost out materials Cost out LSS Supplier DPPM CONC	GQMS policy 13 GQMS policy 15 SS projects Lean savings	QOS plant, controls div Value stream map Profit plan LSS—7 wastes floor level	Monthly QOS Monthly QOS controls div APEX review biannual Monthly cost council review	Comptroller
Strategic Planning	Safety Quality Profitability Customer satisfaction	OCA strategic planning process MESH profit plans value cycle	As defined QOS roadmap	PAIP (GQMS), process summit, council structure and its alignment to QOS metrics	QOS plant and floor level Value stream map Customer focus MESH focus Employee survey Benchmark 8D process	Weekly QOS Monthly QOS All product realization processes reviewed twice a year	OpEx manager

TABLE 5.11

Determine Product and Process Requirements for Each Support Process

Support Processes	Key Requirements	Design Elements	Key Measures	Minimization of Costs	Improvement Process	Review Frequency	Owner
Hydraulic test process	To comply to the customer requirements To assure required function Seek opportunities for process/product improvement	LSS PROLaunch GQMS Customer application	OEE	Set up reduction Training Equipment modification for safety and reduction of test time	Training in hydraulics circuits Certification of test operators Built-in incentive for internal promotion TPM	Test process reviewed twice a year Corrective actions on OEE results	Test engineer
Purchasing–SCM	Component availability Component quality Control inventory Supplier partnership	Supplier viz Consignment/pull system DSS	Supplier OTD Supplier DPPM Cost out	SIOP (sales, inventory, and operations planning) Supplier viz Electronic KanBan LCC sourcing Supplier partnerships—consignment	SIOP MFGPro reports Focus suppliers Supplier viz	Weekly QOS Monthly QOS Six-month review of the process	SCM manager
Training/employee development	Convert qualified employees into capable and skillful employees	Training requirements GQMS Strategic planning OCA	Flex training Customer DPPM LSS score GQMS score	Conversion of qualified employees into competent employees thru training in LSS, GQMS, hydraulic principles and testing, flex training, and APEX	Line leader concept Analysis of training effectiveness	Weekly QOS Monthly QOS Six-month review of the process	HR manager

TABLE 5.12

Key Support Processes Directly Supporting Each Key Value Creation Process

Relationship among Processes	
Key Value Creation Processes	**Key Support Processes**
Assembly	Hydraulic test process
Assemble SICVs and MCDs	Purchasing–SCM
	Training/employee development
Manufacturing	Purchasing–SCM
Manufacture manifolds, components, and hone cages	Training/employee development
Cost Out	Training/employee development
	Purchasing–SCM
Strategic Planning	Training/employee development
	Purchasing–SCM

Step #7

Compile the relationship matrix showing the KSPs directly supporting each KVCP (Table 5.12).

PROLaunch

The term *PROLaunch* stands for **P**rofitable, **R**eliable, and **O**n-Time **Launch** of new products. Another practical method for developing products is Advanced Product Quality Planning (APQP). Both methods lead to delivering a value to all stakeholders and the customer in particular by understanding their wants and fulfilling them.

USE OF AUTO INDUSTRY CORE TOOLS IN DESIGNING PRODUCTS AND PROCESSES

Proper use and application of these tools are essential for customer satisfaction and sustainability of the organization. The implementation of the six core tools as mandated by the automotive industry and globally adopted by aerospace and other high-technology industries like electronics and health care products is briefly explained in this section.

The core tools are as follows:

Advanced Product Quality Planning (APQP)
Failure Mode and Effects Analysis (FMEA)
Control Plan
Production Part or service component Approval Process (PPAP)
Statistical Process Control (SPC)
Measurement System Analysis (MSA)

It may be mentioned that the first three books of these related four books deal with these core tools in detail:

Book 1: *The Global Quality Management System: Improvement through Systems Thinking*
Book 2: *Lean Transformation: Cultural Enablers and Enterprise Alignment*
Book 3: *The Tactical Guide to Six Sigma Implementation*

Here, introduction of the topics is given so that a reader may want to know more from the abovementioned three books and AIAG publications themselves.

APQP involves the management of product/service design and development whose ultimate goal is to deliver a value to all stakeholders and the customer in particular by understanding their wants and fulfilling them.

Five Phases of APQP:

1. Concept initiation/approval
2. Product design program approval
3. Prototype
4. Pilot
5. Launch

1. Concept Initiation/Approval

This phase starts with planning inputs and ends with planning outputs.

The inputs are as follows:
- Voice of the customer
  - Market research (including OEM vehicle timing and volume expectations)
  - Historical warranty and quality information
  - Team experience
- Business plan/marketing strategy
- Product/process benchmark data

- Product/process assumptions
- Product reliability studies
- Customer inputs

The outputs are as follows:

- Design goals
- Reliability and quality goals
- Preliminary bill of materials
- Preliminary process flowchart
- Preliminary listing of special product and process characteristics
- Product assurance plan
- Management support

2. Product Design Program Approval

Inputs are the same as the outputs for Concept Initiation/ Approval phase.

Design outputs:

- Design Failure Mode and Effects Analysis (DFMEA)
- Design for manufacturability (or service offering) and assembly
- Design verification
- Design reviews
- Prototype build—control plan
- Engineering drawings (including math data)
- Engineering specifications
- Material specifications
- Drawing and specification changes

APQP outputs:

- New equipment, tooling, and facilities requirements
- Special product and process characteristics
- Gages/testing equipment requirements
- Team feasibility commitment and management support

3. Prototype

Inputs are the same as the outputs for Product Design Program Approval phase.

Outputs:

- Packaging standards and specifications
- Product/process quality system review
- Process flowchart
- Floor plan layout
- Process Failure Mode and Effects Analysis (PFMEA)
- Characteristics matrix

- Prelaunch control plan
- Process instructions
- Measurement system analysis plan
- Management support
- Preliminary process capability study plan

4. Pilot

Inputs are the same as the outputs for Prototype phase.
Outputs:

- Significant production run
- Measurement systems evaluation
- Preliminary process capability study
- Production part approval
- Production validation testing
- Packaging evaluation
- Production control plan
- Quality planning sign-off and management support

5. Launch

Inputs are the same as the outputs for Prototype phase.
Outputs:

- Reduced variation
- Improved customer satisfaction
- Improved delivery and service
- Effective use of lessons learned/best practice

APQP Pitfalls

- APQP treated as a "Quality Department Responsibility" (it is a company responsibility)
- APQP is a separate process, not integrated into product development
- Key stakeholders brought in late (quality, production, suppliers)
- Milestones and deliverables ignored
- No top management involvement/support

The following tools are covered in *Lean Transformation: Cultural Enablers and Enterprise Alignment* and *The Tactical Guide to Six Sigma Implementation*.

Failure Mode and Effects Analysis (FMEA)
Control Plan

Statistical Process Control (SPC)
Measurement System Analysis (MSA)

PRODUCTION PART APPROVAL PROCESS (PPAP)

The purpose of **PPAP** is to provide evidence that customers' engineering design record and specification requirements are properly understood by the organization and that the organization's manufacturing process has the potential to produce a product consistently meeting these requirements during an actual production run at the quoted production rate.

PPAP Documents Needed for One Production Part

1. Design records
2. Authorized engineering change documents
3. Customer engineering approval
4. Design FMEA
5. Process flow diagrams
6. Process FMEA
7. Control plan
8. Measurement system analysis studies
9. Dimensional results
10. Material/performance test results
11. Initial process study
12. Qualified laboratory documentation
13. Appearance approval report
14. Sample production parts
15. Master samples
16. Checking aids
17. Customer-specific requirements (records)
18. Part submission warrant
19. Bulk material requirements checklist (as required by the bulk production process)

PPAP Process Pitfalls

- PPAP is treated as a separate process, rather than integrated into product development

- Incomplete PPAP
- Assuming that submission levels are at what is required, rather than what is submitted

---

ACQUISITION AND INTEGRATION

Acquisition

This is a growth strategy employed by companies. The main consideration in acquiring a new asset or business is to consider how this asset will make the existing business more valuable, and how will the existing business add value to the asset being bought.

Good acquiring strategy process has the following key steps:

1. Consider acquisition as a company's growth strategy where the main purpose is not to grow big fast, but leverage the new asset to do what it does better.
   - Invest in the core business of the acquired company and expand into related businesses that strengthen its core
2. Use acquisitions to supplement and support competitive advantage.
3. Develop clear organic and inorganic strategies. Organic growth by better organizational capability planning and expanding manufacturing capabilities and inorganic growth by invest/divest portfolio decisions.
4. Define acquisition objectives and the value it will bring to the growth of the company.
5. Plan for opportunity long before an opportunity arises by creating a pipeline of priority acquisition targets, each with a customized investment plan and systematically cultivate relationships with high-priority targets.

Below is an outstanding example of growth of a company through Acquisition and Integration:

Acquisition and Integration is in the DNA of Eaton Corporation. Eaton Corporation was an $8-billion company in 2002 and an $18-billion company in 2010. In 2011, Eaton became a $36-billion company with the acquisition of the Irish company Cooper Industry and became the largest in Eaton's ($16 billion sales revenue, 2011) 101-year history.

The acquisition track:

Eaton believed that the quickest way to grow the business was through acquisitions and, by 1932, began buying companies in the automotive industry; the diversified company changed its name to Eaton Manufacturing Company. In 1937, Eaton became international by opening a manufacturing plant in Canada. In 1958, Eaton Corporation acquired Fuller Manufacturing. The company name changed once again in 1965 to Eaton Yale & Towne, Inc. after the acquisition of Yale & Towne Manufacturing Co. in 1963. Stockholders approved the change to the company's current name in 1971. Eaton Corp. continues its founder's "philosophy" of growth **through acquisition along with divesting businesses** that no longer fit the corporate vision. In 1978, Eaton Corporation acquired Samuel Moore & Company, Kenway Systems, and Cutler-Hammer. One of Eaton's largest acquisitions was the distribution and control business unit of Westinghouse.

Eaton entered a joint venture with Caterpillar Inc. and purchased 51% of I & S operations (now known as Intelligent Switchgear Organization, LLC). This was followed in 2004 by the acquisition of Powerware. The Powerware brand is known for the design and production of medium to large Uninterruptible Power System (UPS) devices. After several years of co-branding UPS products "Eaton|Powerware," the company is switching to the single brand Eaton for all UPS products.

It acquired Aphel Technologies Ltd., a manufacturer of power distribution product for data centers based in Coventry, UK. Shortly after, it added Pulizzi Engineering Inc., a manufacturer of mission critical power distribution based in Santa Ana, California. In late 2007, it acquired the MGE Office Protection Systems division of Schneider Electric, as a result of Schneider's acquisition of APC. A Taiwanese manufacturer, Phoenixtec, was also acquired, giving the company the highest share in the Chinese single-phase UPS market.

Integration

Beware of the following pitfalls of integration:

- **Missed targets**. Companies fail to clearly define the deal's primary sources of value and its key risks. Some acquirers seem to expect the target company's people to integrate themselves. Others do have an integration program team, but they don't get it up and running until the deal closes.

- **Loss of key people**. Waiting too long for a new organizational structure and to put leaders in place may result in talented executives leaving for greener pastures. Also, when companies fail to address cultural matters and issues that deal with how people feel about the new environment, talented people leave.
- **Poor performance**. In some cases, integration takes up too much attention or simply drags on too long, distracting leaders from their main business. In other cases, unplanned actions or poor systems migration leads to confusion with customers and suppliers. Competitors take advantage of such confusion.

Successful integration is always a challenge. Here are seven essential guidelines that can make the task of integration more manageable and lead to the desired result:

1. **Quantify the gain**

   An acquisition needs a clear objective explanation of how it will strengthen the company's core business. For example:
   - "This deal will give us a unique access to attractive new customers and channels."
   - "This deal will make us clear leaders in our markets."
   - "A deal clarifies several important sources of value and liability and guides in the direction leading to a success."

2. **Prepare yourself to the nature of the deal**

   You must be certain whether it is a scale deal or an expansion in the same or a very similar business—or a scope deal—an expansion into a new market, product, or channel.

3. **Resolve the leadership positions and HR issues quickly**

   The new organization should be aligned around the combined products and processes with the new vision for the combined company. People from both organizations who can contribute the most to the new mission and vision should be selected and placed to fill up these top levels as soon as possible to avoid organizational complications from taking place as time goes by.

4. **Start integration activity as soon as the acquisition plan is made public**

   Nominate a confidential select team of individuals to review legal protocols and to study competitive data and intellectual property. This action will help in speeding up the deal.

5. Manage the integration through a very tight time schedule
The checklist of critical activity must lay out a decision roadmap and manage the integration process activities to a strict time schedule.

6. Select the leaders of the integration team to ensure that each decision is made by the right people at the right time with the best available information.

7. Commit to one common culture

I. CAPITAL OPTIMIZATION—DEPLOYING CAPITAL WISELY

Capital Focus

Figure 5.3 shows the four pillars of capital optimization for deploying capital wisely.

Capital in the form of money or assets is the financial strength of an organization, and is assumed to be available for development or investment. As blood sustains life, capital is the lifeblood of every growing business. Companies aspiring to be market leaders must understand the role of capital in all important business decisions, such as:

- Restructuring of the business
- When is the time to sell some of the assets?
- How can one seize the premium acquisition opportunity?

All above decisions need capital and its efficient deployment. Leading financial consultants advise on considering preserving, optimizing, raising, and investing capital so that an organization can meet business challenges and make better decisions about its strategic use of capital.

1. Preservation of capital

The company needs to preserve capital for timely and fast growth. Thus, review your strengths and weaknesses continuously, seek opportunities while avoiding the threats, and evaluate your long-term cash flow, balance sheet, strategy, and markets. Look for strengths and weaknesses. Seek opportunities, but identify risks and guard against value erosion.

PART SUBMISSION WARRANT

Part Name

Part Number

Purchase ~~Order #~~

Eng. ~~Drawing Change Level~~

Date

Safety and/or Government Regulation ☐ Yes ☐ No

Weight _____

Additional Eng. Changes _____ Dated _____

Shown On Drawing # _____

Checking Aid # _____ Eng. Change Level   Dated _____

SUPPLIER MANUFACTURING INFORMATION   **SUBMISSION INFORMATION**

☐ Dimensional ☐ Materials/Function ☐ Appearance

Supplier Name

Customer Name / Div. **GKN Rockford, Inc.**

Street Address

~~**Buyer**~~

City   State / Province   Postal Code

Country

Note: Does this part contain any restricted or reportable substances?   ☐ Yes   ☐ No

Are plastics identified with appropriate ISO marking codes?   ☐ Yes   ☐ No ☐ N/A

Reason For Submission

☐ Initial sample

☐ Correction of Discrepancy

☐ Sub-Supplier or material source change

☐ Engineering Change(s)

FIGURE 5.3
Four pillars of capital optimization.   (*Continued*)

☐ Parts produced at additional location   ☐ Change in Part Processing

☐ Tooling: Transfer, Replacement, Refurbishment, or Additional   ☐ Tooling Inactive

☐ Change to optional construction or equipment   ☐ Other - please specify

Requested Submission Level (check one)

☐ Level 1 - Warrant only submitted.
☐ Level 2 - Warrant with product samples and limited supporting data submitted.
    Family supporting documents supplied on Level 3 PPAP for PN _____ Approved on _____

☐ Level 3 - Warrant with product samples and complete supporting data submitted.
☐ Level 4 - Warrant and other requirements as defined by customer
☐ Level 5 - Warrant with product samples and supporting data reviewed at supplier's manufacturing location.

Submission Results

The results for: ☐ dimensional measurements ☐ material/functional tests ☐ appearance criteria ☐ statistical package

These results meet all drawing and specification requirements: ☐ Yes   ☐ No   (If "No" - explanation required)

Declaration

I hereby affirm that the samples represented by this certification are representative of our parts, have been made to the applicable customer drawings and specifications, and are made from the specified materials on regular production tooling with no operations other than the regular production process. I also certify that documented evidence of such compliance is on file and available for review.
Explanation/Comments: _____

_____ _____ _____ _____
      print name   title   phone   email

FOR CUSTOMER USE ONLY (IF APPLICABLE)

Part warrant disposition:___ Approved___ Rejected___ Interim approval   **Part functional approval:**___ Approved ___ Waived

Customer Name _ **GKN Rockford, Inc.** _ Customer Signature _____ Date _____

Form # 6156   Rev. 05   Date 02/18/09   DAF# 1783

Supplier Authorized Signature _____ Date _____

FIGURE 5.3 (CONTINUED)
Four pillars of capital optimization.

Preservation of capital needs sound cash flow planning, short-term access to credit facilities, or control of costs and engagement with key stakeholders such as suppliers. Debt management through negotiation of various options also helps in the preservation of capital.

2. Optimization of capital

Capital is a scarce and precious commodity. Capital allocations must pass through a rigorous examination, thus making operational efficiency capital precious. Fast-growing companies need a tight grip on the drivers of efficient capital allocation. Greater operational efficiency can release excess cash and working capital.

Good profit is not an assurance against financial crisis and sustainability in the future. Hence, close control of the cash flow is a must.

Capital required by product and services portfolios should be based on their performance. Internal optimal and timely capital requirement as well as strategic capital required against competition should be readily available and not left to chance.

3. Raising capital

An important part of strategic planning should include making investments from the viewpoint of investment bankers and finance companies. The capital providers should see the investment opportunities in your planning. Remaining prepared to avail capital at the lowest possible cost for the long-term and future requirements makes raising capital easier and affordable.

4. Investing/deploying capital

In order to utilize capital in the best possible way, look for opportunities, find them, and take advantage of such opportunities. Wise use of your capital will make capital providers comfortable because of your faster growth. Potential capital providers expect fast-growth companies to make investment decisions supported by in-depth and varied scenario analyses. Communicate sound value propositions with focus on due diligence on the KBDs that matter most.

Another alternative to raise and invest capital is to promote a joint venture or partnership that could satisfy your investment goals without the risks associated with an acquisition.

5. Becoming an excellent organization

Sound capital management will put you in the best position to continue your journey.

As the Excellent Organization diagnostic below shows, your ability to transition from a growing company to a market leader depends on

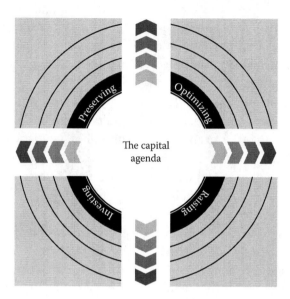

FIGURE 5.4
Attributes of a market leader.

your ability to successfully execute priority tasks in six core business areas:

1. Managing finance
2. Customer focus
3. People focus
4. Risk management
5. Doing business with others
6. Operational excellence

Figure 5.4 is an "all-inclusive" list of attributes of a market leader.

II. WORKING CAPITAL OPTIMIZATION STRATEGY

Capital needed in running a business bleeds away because of the following reasons:

- Most accounts receivable and invoice settlement processes are elaborate and are being manually controlled, thus consuming more time, keeping capital tied down.

- Order-to-cash cycle takes 60 to 120 days on average.
- To shorten the invoice payment time, the popular incentive scheme is "2% 10, net 30." This indicates that a 2% discount can be taken by the buyer only if payment is received in full within 10 days of the date of the invoice, and that full payment is expected within 30 days. For example, if a $1000 invoice has the terms, "2% 10, net 30," the buyer can take a 2% discount ($1000 × 0.02 = $20) and make a payment of $980 within 10 days or pay the full $1000 within the remainder of the 30 days. But most of the time this does not work because some invoices get stuck in internal approvals by the time they reach accounts payable.
- Nearly a third of the invoices involve "exceptional processing"; they don't state a PO number. Such invoices need manual processing, and this takes more than double time to process, thus resulting in increased cost of the transaction.

Cash Management in the AP/AR Process

Efficient management of cash involved in accounts receivables and accounts payables can effectively reduce operating costs and free up the cash. Working capital, if saved, can be put to more productive use.

Most small- and medium-sized organizations follow traditional processes that involve costs of printing and mailing paper checks and stop payment instructions. Reissue of checks, lost checks, and fraud drain the working capital significantly. Manual processing causes lack of visibility and uncertainty around payments, and the suppliers end up maintaining excess cash to safeguard against uncertainty. The working capital tied up in the order-to-cash cycle is sometimes so severe that the suppliers need to rely on expensive financing options at high short-term interest.

Use of Technology in Managing Working Capital

The technology available today plays a major role in helping buyers and suppliers. Automated financial processes enable cost-saving efficiencies and working capital optimization.

6

Human Resource Focus

HUMAN RESOURCE (HR) PROCESSES

Figure 6.1 shows the hierarchy of HR processes.

UNDERSTAND STRATEGIC DIRECTIVES AS LAID OUT IN STRATEGIC PLANNING

Understand the Organization's Philosophy

So far, we have discussed Strategic Directives as laid down in strategic planning (Chapter 3). We have also discussed organizational philosophy toward HR in leadership (Chapter 2). Now, let us understand how cultures are important in HR management.

Understanding Regional Cultures

In addition to the ethnic culture, we are born into a regional culture. Life experiences are largely based on the geographical area where one is raised. A region could be

- A group of states, such as the religion of "The Bible Belt" in the United States (known for its strong Christian beliefs) or southern states of India with their strong religious traditions
- An entire state, like the gambling culture of Nevada or a military culture of Rajputs in India
- Parts of a state, Michigan's Upper Peninsula versus Detroit for example or Saurashtra versus south Gujarat

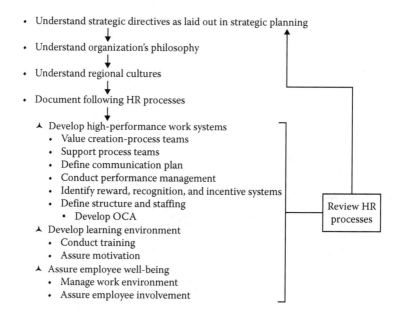

FIGURE 6.1
HR processes.

- A city, considering the cultures specific to Boston or specific to Ahmedabad in Gujarat

Because of the transient nature of society, regional cultural traits are picked up originally from our parents and then modified or added to as we move from one region to another.

The most common regional culture is one's nationality. People share experiences and learn to react in certain ways based on their nation. Overlay that with state or provincial cultures and you begin to see the complexity of this cultural distinction.

MANY DIMENSIONS OF CULTURAL ASSIMILATION

Cultural assimilation:

- An employee's ability to fit within an organization's culture is one dimension of cultural assimilation.

- It also means how an employee fits with customers, outside vendors, and other company associates.
- It refers to the geographic aspects of culture as well. In today's global economy, it takes on a greater meaning.

FIT IS A NECESSITY

The ability to "fit" within an organization is recognized as an essential aspect contributing to employee success. It is a major factor in the recruiting process. In fact, the cultural fit can become the deciding factor in whether an executive is chosen for a job over competitors.

FIT IS ESSENTIAL

The ability to "fit" within an organization has come to be recognized as an essential component contributing to employee success. It is also a major factor in the hiring process.

In fact, in a recent global survey of recruiters conducted by the executive search firm Korn/Ferry International, cultural fit was found to be a deciding factor in whether an executive is chosen for a job over competitors.

DEVELOP HIGH-PERFORMANCE WORK SYSTEMS

- a. Value creation-process teams
- b. Support process teams
- c. Define communication plan
- d. Conduct performance management
- e. Identify reward systems
- f. Define structure and staffing
- g. Develop Organizational Capability Assessment (OCA)

TABLE 6.1

Communication Plan

Communication Method	Frequency	Owner
Intranet system	As required	IT manager
Bulletin boards general	Monthly	HR manager
Bulletin boards department	Monthly	Functional manager
MESH system	Monthly	ISO140001 leader
Bulletin boards shop floor metrics	Monthly	Production supervisors
LSS activities	As required	LSS coordinator
Round table meeting	Monthly	Staff
Performance review	Yearly	Management
Midyear performance review	Yearly	Management
Departmental meetings	Monthly	Management
Management meetings	As required	HR manager
Goals and objectives	Annually	Staff

a. Value Creation Process Teams

We have covered this item in Chapter 5 under "Work Councils."

b. Support Process Teams

We have covered this item in Chapter 5 under "Work Councils."

c. Define Communication Plan

Communication plan is shown in Table 6.1.

d. Conduct Performance Management

APEX (Achieving Performance Excellence) Process

APEX is the key component of the overall performance management process that is used to support high-performance work for salaried employees. All employees participate in APEX, which includes establishing goals and identifying development needs. Each leader has goals established in APEX that are linked to the company president. The goals are focused on the achievement of the sales performance, profit performance, and OCA. Goals are communicated and cascaded down (Figure 6.2) to the direct reports and functional leaders within the organization at the annual HO Leadership Meeting. Each salaried employee's goals are linked to the

2005 Goal Alignment and Personal Goal Commitment

2013 CEO	
2013 VP Manufacturing	
2013 Engineering Manager	Goal

Culture

Ensure the Leadership system is based on BS principles and drives a passionate and performance-driven culture based on an empowered and well-trained workforce that delivers an overall satisfaction score of 4.10 on the customer annual survey and a score of 3.75 on the overall dimension of manager effectiveness. The annual survey will be supplemented with a PWP assessment that delivers an assessed score of 2.0 in 2005.

Create and successfully execute a plan to build organizational strength by developing employees in the Quality area.	4.1
Improve external customer satisfaction through quick RMA/QAR response.	3.75

Improve external customer satisfaction through quick RMA/QAR response.

Meet all campus EHS/Safety objectives in terms of training and responsiveness.	2.0

Create a culture that every Council and every floor team is measured and rated on their performance and recognized for their contributions through the plant employee recognition system.

Leverage leadership in Quality Council to drive results and recognition.

Delivery

Create a systematic delivery system in Reynosa that improves 2005 first half delivery performance to 90% OTD (on-time delivery) to MADD, and 2005 second half delivery performance to 95% to MADD. Create special emphasis through the customer care process, and the tracking of Distributor OTD and ensure that Distributor OTD exceeds the OEM OTD to support PGT planning for shift in channel mix.

Take part in supplier development projects to improve supplier OTD to reduce the shortages.	Q2—90%, Q4—95%

Utilization of LSS principles to reduce Reynosa DOH (days on hand) to 37. This will be done through the expansion of consigned inventory and the elimination of 1.5 DOH of WIP.

Limit inventory to < $40K at any time.	<$40K

Continue driving the Lean Journey as evidenced by a score of 3.5 to the new LSS criteria by March 31, 2005. In addition, create at least two cellular flow cells and self-assess to 3.75 by the end of 2005.

FIGURE 6.2

Cascaded goals. *(Continued)*

Be a Leader for Error-proofing, TPM, and Set Up Reduction and obtain a score of >4 average in these three tools.	4.30

Drive Reynosa 2013 Customer DPPM to 300 DPPM by December 2013.

Improve External Customer DPPM from 475 to 300 DPPM.	300 DPPM
Improve Supplier DPPM from 4890 to 2700 DPPM.	2700 DPPM
Improve Final test failure rate from 4.5% in 2012 to 3.6% in 2013.	3.6%
Improve Product RTY to 99.379% = 4 Sigma = 6210 DPPM.	6210 DPPM
Provide leadership to improve value creation and support processes.	

Create Partnership with Design group and customer service to deliver ISO/TS 16949 certificate for new product line.

Obtain ISO/TS 16949 Certification in June/July 2013.	Certify in TS

Modify current QOS system to comply with the GQMS system and attain an assessed score of 100% on Phase 1 target and 70% on Phase 2 targets by the end of 2013.

Implement Phase 1 and Phase 2 of the GQMS with an assessment score of >80%.	85%

Growth/ Profitability

Partnership with SCM (Supply Chain Management) to hit $1.390 million of material cost out and deliver in-plant lean savings of $302K to hit 2013 plan cost out target of $1.692 million.

Leverage prototype manifold machining to hit planned financial goal of $1.692 million.	

Hit incremental/decremental plan target of 32%.

Control departmental check book not to exceed the budget.	

Integrate Vinita Assembly Operations in Reynosa matching premove baselines in Customer DPPM and Customer OTD. These will be accomplished with a leveraged salary structure that will hit the plan headcount target without the addition of company heads.

Provide quality/process leadership in this project as measured by attaining all OTD, DPPM, and financial targets.	

Provide detail planning to support the transfer of Project Captain and hit product material cost down target of $1.9 million.

Provide quality and process support to project to ensure success as measured by attaining financial target.	

FIGURE 6.2 (CONTINUED)
Cascaded goals.

overall goals of the organization through APEX. Once goals are established and cascaded throughout HO, employees are expected to perform against their goals and are rewarded.

Cascaded Goals

An example of cascaded goals from the president, to the VP of manufacturing, to the engineering/quality manager is shown in Figure 6.2.

APEX Plan

1. Goal Setting
    Review expectations and priorities with manager.
    Set SMART goals.
2. Competencies
    Know which competencies apply to your role.
    Select functional competencies as applicable.
3. Development Plans
    On the basis of development needs, performance coaching plans are initiated.
    The performance coaching process consists of six steps:
    1. Set the stage
    2. Agree on the standard or ideal
    3. Agree on the actual performance
    4. Determine the cause
    5. Take action
    6. Follow up

1. Set the Stage

The opening comments of the person who initiated the meeting should clearly state **the purpose of the meeting**. For example, "I'm concerned that project X is behind schedule. We're meeting to see if problems exist and, if so, what we can do about them" or "I thought my presentation went well. We're meeting to discuss what went especially well, what went less well, and how my next presentation can be even better." If your manager initiated the meeting, you can help set the stage for a productive meeting by practicing the skill of active listening.

Tips for Active Listening

- Maintain eye contact and calm body language.
- Don't interrupt.
- Don't just listen to the words; listen to the feelings and meaning.
- Test your understanding by paraphrasing or summarizing what you heard before you respond.
- Ask questions to clarify or confirm your understanding.
- Acknowledge his or her feelings. Use statements such as "You seem frustrated about the delays."
- State your own feelings. Feelings and emotions need to be dealt with before dealing with the content of the discussion.
- Active listening by you and your manager will result in a more open, comfortable, productive meeting. It's important to create this climate during the first step of the process.

2. Agree on the Standard or Ideal

A frequent cause of performance issues is a difference in expectations. When a manager says "Get back to me as soon as possible," he or she may be thinking before the end of the day, and you may be thinking before the end of the week. When an issue exists because of different standards, simply clarifying the standard may be all that is required to eliminate the issue. When the purpose of performance coaching is not to correct an issue but to improve a process or review lessons learned after completing a project, you still must define the standard, the expected results, or the ideal. For example, before discussing ways to improve a presentation, first discuss "What would an ideal presentation look like?" By agreeing on the standard or ideal, you have a framework for discussing actual performance. To help you agree on a standard, you may want to refer to your criteria for setting goals and expectations in your performance and development plans.

3. Agree on the Actual Performance

When the purpose of performance coaching is to solve an issue, four useful questions to ask are as follows:

1. What is the issue?
2. Where is the issue?
3. When does the issue happen?
4. How big is the issue?

It is also useful to define what the issue is not. For example, if project X is behind schedule but project Y is not, then the cause must be something unique to project X. When the purpose of performance coaching is not to discuss an issue but rather to "discuss what we learned from this experience," don't answer the "what, where, when" questions. Instead, use the characteristics of ideal performance to direct your analysis or simply consider the following:

- "What went best?"
- "What went least well?"
- "What were the strengths and weaknesses?"

In any event, always discuss "What happened?"—the actual performance—before discussing ways to improve performance.

4. Determine the Cause

The most effective and efficient actions to eliminate an issue are those that address its cause. Comparing what the issue is and is not usually prompts specific questions that lead to the cause. For example, why project X but not project Y? When the purpose of performance coaching is to debrief or to learn from a recently completed assignment, comparing what went best with what went least well often leads to insights and specific improvement ideas.

5. Take Action

The purpose of performance coaching is to take action to improve performance. The temptation is to jump straight to the "take action" step. This rarely works. By first discussing the standard, the actual performance, and the cause, you are better prepared to take effective actions. A productive way to identify possible solutions is to brainstorm with your manager. Simply generate a large number of possible actions. Don't argue. Don't agree or disagree. Don't evaluate the ideas. Frequently ask, "What's another idea?" After generating a large number of ideas (6 to 20, depending on the situation), test each idea against the cause and against other criteria you agree to use to evaluate the ideas.

Once you agree on the actions, create a specific plan for implementing each one. Put in writing "who will do what by when."

6. Follow Up

Agree on ways to measure improvement. Then, schedule a time to meet with your manager to review progress so you can modify the plan if it is not working or to celebrate success if it is.

APEX Plan Execution

1. Tracking and Monitor Progress
   - Keep notes
   - Inform manager of progress and challenges
2. Midyear Progress Check
   - Submit progress
   - Discuss progress with manager
   - Continue tracking and monitor progress

APEX Plan Evaluation

Figure 6.3 shows Performance Evaluation Workflow.

- Performance evaluation
- Self-evaluation
- Manager evaluation
- Functional manager
- Second-level approval

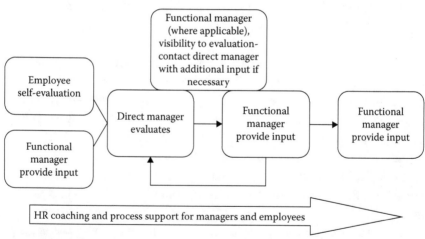

Performance is assessed best with input from multiple sources. The APEX process integrates input from the employee's self-evaluation, the employee's functional manager (where applicable), direct supervisor, and second level manager.

FIGURE 6.3
Performance Evaluation Workflow.

e. Identify Reward, Recognition, and Incentive Systems

The process includes compensation strategies, recognition programs, and incentives. It is targeted toward reinforcing a high-performance, customer, and business focus through the deployment of merit increases, executive incentive compensation, sales incentive compensation, stock options, the Star Points program, and various localized compensation strategies and recognition plans. The merit increase process is championed by the president and the HR director to ensure alignment between the performance ratings and the merit pay increase. This analysis is conducted for all salaried employees. Executive and sales incentive payments are directly tied to successful achievement of business goals. An annual calibration meeting for all employees participating in executive incentive compensation is conducted by the HR director and championed by the president.

Stock options are used to retain and motivate employees at certain levels with additional options offered to individuals who perform at exemplary levels during the year.

The Star program is one avenue for rewarding employees for outstanding achievement.

f. Define Structure and Staffing and Develop OCA

Skills needed by potential employees are identified by the job design process, the strategic plan, and OCA.

Human capital plans are developed in the OCA, on the basis of the needs identified in the strategic plan. This includes planning for skills needed for key strategic business plans on a global basis. There are numerous examples of this in the OCA, such as

- Hiring a sales leader for South Africa to accelerate turnaround.
- Determining the sales and marketing structure in Asia and developing a staffing plan (speed the growth in Asia).
- Continuing to execute global engineering footprint with emphasis on recruiting electromechanical process control experienced engineers, software engineers, and electronics engineers for new product development.
- First preference is given to existing staff that have necessary qualifications, recorded achievements, and experience. This promotes retention of valued employees.

OCA Process

- HR management establishes process for organizational capability review
- HR educates senior management on the process and timeline
- Each facility and function performs assessment of leadership capability with ties to strategic plan
- HR manager leads discussion of organizational capability at staff meeting
- HR manager rolls up plant and functional reviews
- HR manager and VP/GM analysis of senior management to identify organizational strengths and development needs is completed
- Formal presentations conducted with senior VP and CEO to review action and succession plans. Gaps identified
- Action plans prepared to address gaps
- Final presentations conducted with senior VP and CEO to review action and succession plans
- Action plans reviewed and processes improved

An example of an OCA survey of the engineering manager by the HR manager is shown in Table 6.2.

Develop Learning Environment

- Conduct training
- Assure motivation

CONDUCT TRAINING

The approach to education, training, and development is driven by requirements in the strategic planning, OCA, and the performance management process. Other inputs include government and regulatory requirements, company requirements (including components of Business System Excellence), customer requirements, local goals, the safety policy, and analysis of individual development plans in APEX or OCA. Each location's HR manager is responsible for analyzing training needs, developing the local training plan, monitoring the training plan, and evaluating the effectiveness of the training. Once the strategic plan's key business

TABLE 6.2

OCA Survey by the HR Manager

Function/Question	Quality	Engineering	Lean Six Sigma	Design	Maintenance	Tooling
Who are the top performers in your plant/department?	Quality manager	Engineering manager	Six Sigma Black Belt	Design manager	Maintenance manager	Tool room superintendent
How strong is your staff? (strong/average/weak)	Strong	Strong	Strong	Strong	Strong	Strong
Who are the top performers on your staff?	Employees X, Y, and Z					
Who needs to improve?	Employees A and B					
Who, if anyone, is your possible successor?	Employees X and Z					
Who is likely to be your successor?	Employee X					

Note: Empty cells are filled up in a similar manner after due diligence and performance evaluation.

initiatives are established, then gaps in education and training necessary to meet objectives are identified and included in the OCA process.

ASSURE MOTIVATION

The Global Quality Management System: Improvement through Systems Thinking and *Lean Transformation: Cultural Enablers and Enterprise Alignment* referred here extensively deal with motivation. However, it is crucial to guard against "alienation." Sense of estrangement felt by employees is reflected in their lack of warmth toward the organization and in believing that their job/work is not meaningful to other aspects of their lives. Alienation is caused commonly by factors such as a lack of involvement in even basic decision making, lack of human contact, little hope for betterment, and a feeling of powerlessness.

ASSURE EMPLOYEE WELL-BEING

- Manage work environment
- Assure employee involvement

The key factors that affect employee well-being and satisfaction are primarily identified in the company philosophy and its work practices.
Feedback is provided by

- The Employee Engagement Survey process
- The communication plan process
- Exit interviews

The Employee Engagement Survey process is carried by teams called "Friends of the company."

These teams maintain right communication and promote employee involvement through a round table meeting.

The shop floor level representatives meet once a month over a sponsored lunch and discuss the following aspects relating to their involvement in company's activities:

1. Security
2. Respect and equality
3. Favoritism
4. Support at work
5. Development skills
6. Motivation, program ideas
7. Information and tools
8. Manufacturing process
9. Most important clients
10. Boards Quality Operating System (QOS)
11. Organizational communication plans
12. Job training
13. Teamwork
14. Recognition programs
15. Job satisfaction

The discussion ends by assessing the level of involvement by rating the activities on a 1–5 scale.

A typical result may look like the example below:

Safety	4.78
Supervisors	4.35
Processes	4.33
Communication	4.42
Teamwork	4.67
Recognition	4.33
Job satisfaction	4.78

As can be seen, the lowest three ratings are for process improvement, supervisor contribution, and recognition. Observations for improvement are made and the actions taken are reported by the management at the next round table employee meeting.

FINAL THOUGHT

In times of rapid and complex global changes, there is a need to foster a more creative organization. But the main obstacle is usually the structure of the organization. The traditional command-and-control model, based on a chain of command with orders being passed down the chain and managers reporting back up the chain, is not suitable for most organizations. This structure creates intransigence (lack of understanding and an uncompromising attitude). New ideas coming from lower levels in this hierarchy are seen as having lower value, largely because those ideas are not understood at high levels or were not developed there. The authoritative attitude strangles new ideas as they rise through the chain of command. Organizations have recognized this problem and have attempted to overcome it through various approaches, such as engagement, empowerment, and motivation, but the problem persists. Attempts to integrate creativity into business strategy will fail unless structure is addressed with strategic HR planning as covered in this chapter.

7

Measurement, Analysis, and Knowledge Management

The **Measurement, Analysis, and Knowledge Management** Category examines how your organization selects, gathers, analyzes, manages, and improves its data, information, and knowledge assets. Also examined is how your organization reviews its performance.

The main point within the criteria is that all key information should be gathered and analyzed to measure performance effectively and manage the organization. In simplest terms, this category is the "brain center" for the alignment of an organization's operations with its strategic directions. However, since information and analysis might themselves be primary sources of competitive advantage and productivity growth, the category also includes such strategic considerations.

1. How does the organization select its data to support operational performance and strategic decision making and innovation?
   a. The selection of the required data stems from the organization's vision, mission, Key Business Drivers (KBDs), and strategic planning.
   b. KBDs are defined first. They give rise to Key Performance Indicators (KPIs) and lead to Key Support Measures (KSMs).
   c. Results tracking data are the foundation through which the daily, weekly, and monthly data are collected.
2. How does the organization gather its data?
   a. As shown in Figure 7.1, the data are collected by the four councils: safety and culture, quality, speed, and cost and growth. They track the data (19 types of data shown) through the result tracker work instructions, forms, and digital devices like a personal digital assistant, also known as a handheld PC.

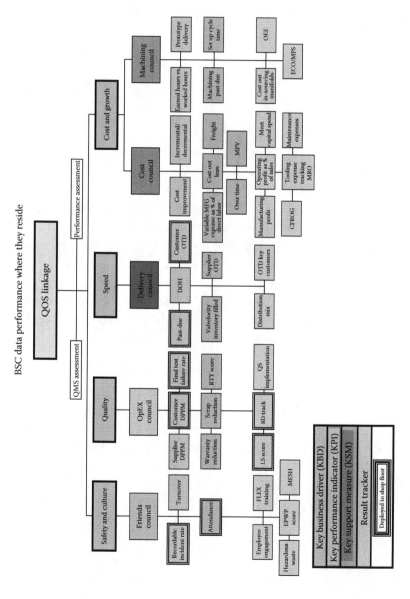

FIGURE 7.1
Balanced Scorecard measures.

3. How does the organization analyze and review its performance?
   a. The data are first collected in the Balanced Scorecard (Table 7.1) where the data trend is determined.
   b. Weekly Quality Operating System (QOS) meetings held by the councils review the data and using the Performance Analysis and Improvement Process (PAIP) (Figure 7.2)
      i. Ensure the quality and availability of data and information to those who need it
      ii. Review organizational performance and capabilities
      iii. Manage organizational knowledge using corporate software standards
4. Information technology and corporate software standards
   a. Production, projects, budgets, and schedule are easily maintained when procedures are working and if they are based on standards. Software standards have proven concepts and the standards requirements when implemented make the delivery process more efficient by reducing costs and increasing scope and quality. The standards promote quality and efficiency; they create more efficient and predictable software products, providing a tool for consistency, confidence, and faster communication.
5. Assessment of the business excellence system
   a. Chapter 9 deals with the Business Excellence Assessment System.

This process starts at the highest level, with the senior leaders identifying a set of metrics that will be used for monitoring overall organizational performance. A balanced set of metrics is identified. An important part of this step is reviewing metrics selected from the previous year and identifying adjustments to better align the measurement process with organizational needs and direction.

Excellent organizations describe how they review organizational performance and capabilities. Their senior leaders participate in these reviews. They document policy and the process for performance analysis and improvement.

TABLE 7.1

Balanced Scorecard—A Typical Example

Scorecard Metric	Description of Metric (This Column Explains How Metric Is Arrived at)	2012 Actual Past Year	2013 Actual	Jan 13 Record Data at the End of Each Month	2013 Goal
Total sales ($,000)	Total $$ of product or services purchased by customers during the reporting period	$48,081	$53,133	Fill in actual data for each month in the next columns	$68,000
Past due shipments ($,000 past due)	Total $$ of all shipments (internal and external customers) that are past due at the end of the month	$665	$502		$150
Mix (% distribution sales)	Percentage of all orders that are associated with distribution customers (typically higher margin sales)	26%	26%		22%
Customer Satisfaction/Quality					
Customer returns (Defective Parts per Million [DPPM])	Ratio of total plant verified customer returns reported in the month to total units sold during the month expressed in "parts per million." Formula: (# verified units rejected at customer facility/# units shipped) × 1,000,000. Note: Units that are analyzed and found to not be the responsibility of the company are excluded from this calculation	457	490		400

(Continued)

TABLE 7.1 (CONTINUED)

Balanced Scorecard—A Typical Example

Scorecard Metric	Description of Metric (This Column Explains How Metric Is Arrived at)	2012 Actual Past Year	2013 Actual	Jan 13 Record Data at the End of Each Month	2013 Goal
On-time delivery (% to MADD)	MADD = mutually agreed due date. On-time delivery to the customer is defined as: % of line items shipped "on-time" to mutually agreed upon ship date (or customer request date if no agreed upon date). Formula: (total # of line items shipped "on-time" during the month/total # of line items due to ship during the month) × 100	83.1%	89.0%		95.0%
Final test failure rate (DPPM)		45,870	27,288		0
Scrap (as % of sales)		0.29%	0.25%		0.20%
Innovation					
Cost improvement ($,000)	Total value of all cost out categories	$700	$743		$900
Lean Six Sigma savings ($,000)		$338	$802		$1800
Material savings ($,000)		$362	$491		$500
Lean 8 tools—score	Latest Lean system score (validated)	3.3	3.6		4.5

(Continued)

TABLE 7.1 (CONTINUED)

Balanced Scorecard—A Typical Example

Scorecard Metric	Description of Metric (This Column Explains How Metric Is Arrived at)	2012 Actual Past Year	2013 Actual	Jan 13 Record Data at the End of Each Month	2013 Goal
Cycle Time					
Total Inventory—Days on Hand	Gross inventories at the end of the current month	39.4	35.0		30.0
Suppliers					
Supplier quality (DPPM)	(No. of defective units)/(total no. of units received) × 1,000,000	4980	2557		1800
Supplier delivery (% on-time)	Percentage of line items received "on-time" within the reporting period. On-time is defined as being 2 days early to 0 days late. This applies to all suppliers (internal and external). Formula: (no. of line items on time in a month/no. of line items due in a month) × 100	90.6%	94.0%		98.0%
Employee Satisfaction					
Safety (recordable incident rate)		0.00	0.00		0.00
Philosophy and work practices score					0.0

(Continued)

TABLE 7.1 (CONTINUED)

Balanced Scorecard—A Typical Example

Scorecard Metric	Description of Metric (This Column Explains How Metric Is Arrived at)	2012 Actual Past Year	2013 Actual	Jan 13 Record Data at the End of Each Month	2013 Goal
Employee training delivered (Year to Date %)					98%
Management of environment safety and health assessment (% of policies >55%)					70%
Business Excellence					
Cost of nonconformance (% of sales)	The cost of nonconformance for a location (specific accounting categories defined on data tab)				0.0%
Incremental/decremental ($,000)	Performance in $ above/below expected profit based on incremental/decremental sales	($1505)	($3010)		$0
Cash flow	Annualized cash flow result as reported from financial reports	21.50%	3.90%		0.00%
Manufacturing profit (% of sales)	Manufacturing profit divided by net sales expressed as a percentage	13.40%	13.30%		15.00%
Suppliers					
Rolled throughout yield (RTY%)					0.0%
Prototype delivery (% on-time)					0%

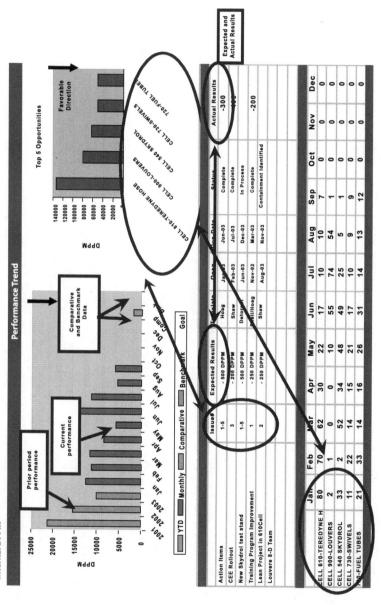

FIGURE 7.2
PAIP guide.

PERFORMANCE ANALYSIS AND IMPROVEMENT PROCESS (PAIP)

1. Scope

This procedure describes the minimum requirements and controls for ensuring that organizations systematically implement the PAIP. This policy applies to all levels of the organization (corporate, groups, operations, divisions, and sites) and all areas of the business.

2. Policy

2.1 The top management team for the site will meet at least twice annually, to review and update the strategic plan initiatives, projects, and goals to ensure that the plan complies and aligns with the corporate strategic plan.

2.2 The approved strategic plan shall be communicated and available to all affected managers.

2.3 All levels of management (executive to shop floor) shall develop plans; determine the key processes and key measurements (preferably having leading data), with related performance standards and continuous improvement goals for their areas of responsibility; in line with the focus and objectives of the strategic plan.

2.4 Tracking methods shall be created to track the key measurements for the manager's respective area of responsibility. Tracking via trend analysis and Pareto and Paynter charts is strongly recommended, including action plans as appropriate.

2.5 Periodic meetings (minimum quarterly) shall be conducted to review the measurements by the managers for corporate, group, operations, division, business unit, plant, department, and work cell. Performance of the measurements shall be tracked at the designated frequency. Action plans shall be generated for metrics that are not trending toward the desired goal. Structured problem-solving method, such as the 8 Disciplines (8D) process, will be used to determine the root cause and develop corrective actions for items that are underperforming. Employees at all levels will be involved, as applicable, to facilitate the improvement process. Minutes of the meeting shall be tracked.

2.6 Correlation between the metrics and the final stakeholder desired results shall periodically (minimum twice annually) be established and reviewed as part of the management review process. Metrics and goals will be adjusted as required to adapt to the changing business requirements.

PERFORMANCE ANALYSIS AND IMPROVEMENT PROCESS FLOW

As we can see, the PAIP covers total organizational excellence in Figure 7.3.

Keeping constant employee awareness for excellence in the center and based on stakeholder feedback, a strategic plan is prepared. Organizational key value creation, support, and administrative processes are identified. These processes are measured by the measures shown in Figure 7.1. These measures (KBDs, KPIs, KSMs, and tracker data) are improved by applying

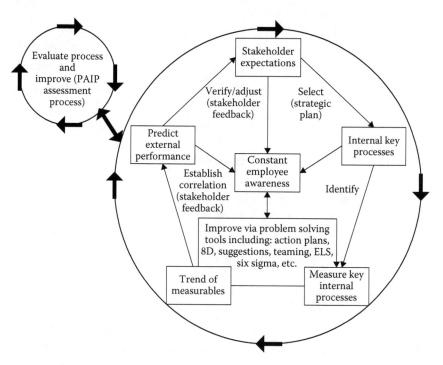

FIGURE 7.3
PAIP flow.

problem-solving tools and methods including action plans, 8D, suggestions, teamwork, and Enterprise Lean Six Sigma. The resulting trends are measured, the correlation is established between stakeholder expectations and actual results, and finally considering stakeholder feedback, the next strategic plan is prepared taking the organization to higher levels of excellence.

INFORMATION AND KNOWLEDGE MANAGEMENT

Information Technology (IT)

IT plays a major role in the measurement, analysis, and knowledge management.

Information technology has transformed the way businesses operate and interact with their key stakeholders: employees, suppliers, customers, and investors. From desktops and mobile devices to business servers and powerful search engines, IT helps businesses manage daily operations, control costs, and compete with large and established companies.

IT comprises of six main functions.

1. Communication

IT enables efficient and high-speed communications. E-mail, teleconferencing, video conferencing, and Internet calling allow employees to stay in touch with their colleagues around the world. IT also enables virtual collaboration. For example, U.S. employees can conduct product design meetings with their Chinese or Indian colleagues using video conferencing. Employees can log into their company servers from home, and traveling managers can respond to e-mails or download documents using mobile technologies. Companies can also set up internal social media sites that allow employees to exchange information and collaborate on projects.

2. Data Management

Data management is a key IT function. Technological advances and increasingly complex businesses have increased text, voice, and video data traffic within and among organizations. Businesses use databases to store, manage, and access vast amounts of data, including customer information, inventory records, employee files, and financial documents. However, small and large businesses must guard against unauthorized accesses, which may compromise data integrity and raise privacy concerns.

3. Marketing

IT is increasingly central to a company's marketing operations. These may include creating advertising copy on powerful graphics computers, placing ads on social media sites, and processing online orders on an e-commerce site. Small business owners can use online search engines to research consumer buying trends and identify profitable marketing opportunities. Software systems also allow companies to track visits on websites, clicks on Internet ads, and the amount of time spent on each section of an e-commerce site.

4. Process Improvement

Companies can leverage IT to improve processes and achieve cost savings. For example, a small business could insist on paperless communication inside the company to save on printing and duplication costs, while achieving reliable data transfer. Virtual collaboration saves on expensive travel costs and improves productivity because employees do not have to spend hours or days on planes and at airport terminals. IT can make human resource processes more efficient. For example, a small business can organize Internet-based training sessions for its customers and employees, thus saving cost and time.

5. Enterprise Resource Planning

Enterprise Resource Planning (ERP) is the use of software systems to link together business functions, including sales, manufacturing, human resources, and accounting. Management gets access to real-time aggregated information, which helps in operational and strategic decision making. For large companies, these systems can be expensive and the installation can disrupt operations for months. However, small businesses can install the software modules for one function at a time, thus minimizing costs and disruptions.

IT implements several processes to ensure that data and information availability mechanisms are kept current with changing business needs and directions.

Examples are as follows:

- IT strategic planning process
- IT employee satisfaction survey
- IT customer satisfaction survey
- IT supplier performance evaluation resource
- IT help desk request process

6. Cloud ERP

It is an approach to ERP that makes use of cloud computing platforms and services to provide a business with more flexible business process transformation.

ERP is an industry term for the broad set of activities that helps a business manage the important parts of its business such as purchasing and inventory management. ERP applications can also include modules for the finance and human capital management aspects of a business.

To some industry experts, the promise of cloud computing is that it will provide an opportunity for business to completely transform how it uses and pays for information technology. For example, cloud sourcing legacy ERP applications might eliminate the need for a business to purchase the necessary server and storage hardware and maintain it on site, which, in turn, has the potential to reduce operational expenditures. Other industry experts, however, point out that the problems associated with ERP software deployments—such as integration problems between ERP modules and a company's legacy systems—would simply transfer to the cloud.

The hope is that ERP software developed specifically for cloud computing environments will include new feature sets that were simply not possible using old technology. Until then, cloud ERP is seen as being good for start-up organizations and new business divisions within an existing company.

8

Business Results Focus

The Business Results Category 7 provides results focus that encompasses an organization's

- Objective evaluation
- Customers' evaluation of the organization's products and services
- Overall financial and market performance
- Human resource results
- Leadership system and social responsibility
- Results of all key processes and process improvement activities

Through this focus, the criteria maintain

- Superior value of offerings as viewed by the organization's customers and the marketplace.
- Superior organizational performance as reflected in operational, human resources, legal, ethical, and financial indicators, as well as organizational and personal learning.
- Chapter 8 thus provides "real-time" information (measures of progress) for evaluation and improvement of processes, products, and services, in alignment with overall organizational strategy. PAIP calls for analysis and review of business results data and information to determine your overall organizational performance.

The graphs that follow are real-life examples. Studies and extracting actionable projects from trends, comparison with benchmark, and position among others in the industry are important to lead the organization to be the best.

BUSINESS CATEGORY RESULTS

Product, Service, and Customer-Focused Results

- Figure 8.1: Customer Relationship and Review (CRR) Data
  - The CRR process measures five key indicators:
    - Quality
    - Value
    - Delivery
    - Understanding of customer needs
    - Innovation
  - The historical data show higher ratings from OEMs for delivery and understanding needs.
- Figure 8.2: Customer quality (DPPM) shows
  - Maintaining improvement despite new challenges (new operations)
- Figure 8.3: On-time delivery (OTD) data show
  - Organizational performance as compared to OTD data from
    - Best competitor
    - Best in the class
    - Industry average
- Figure 8.4: Schedule adherence (sales backlog)
  - The graph shows a steady progress in a multiproduct, multicomponent, and small batch quantity production. This was made possible partly because of Lean implementation.

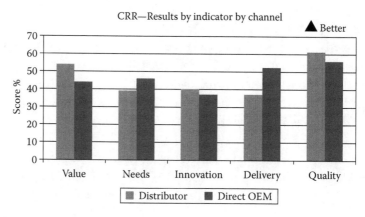

FIGURE 8.1

Customer Relationship Review results.

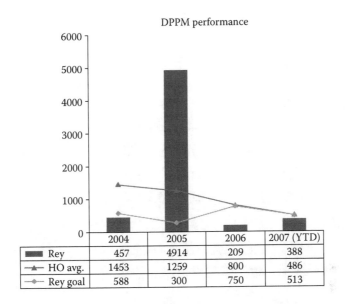

FIGURE 8.2
Customer DPPM.

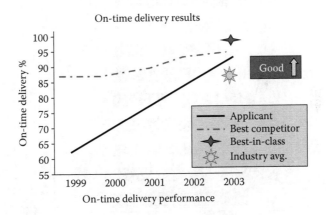

FIGURE 8.3
OTD performance.

Market Results

- Figure 8.5: Market share growth—HO global
  - The data show improving market share trend among peers.
- Figure 8.6: Response to product claims
  - The data track and measure response time to close a product claim as a measure of customer satisfaction.

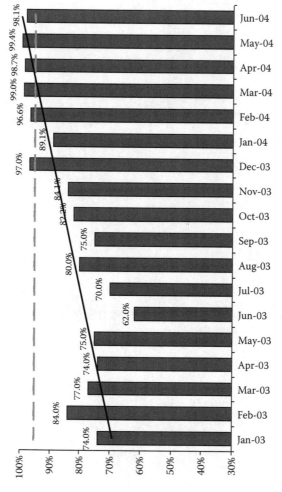

RH schedule adherence by month *vs.* goal
(production attainment of schedule)

	1/03	2/03	3/03	4/03	5/03	6/03	7/03	8/03	9/03	11/03	12/03	1/04	3/04	4/04	6/04
Actual	74.0%	84.0%	77.0%	74.0%	75.0%	62.0%	70.0%	80.0%	75.0%	84.1%	97.0%	89.1%	99.0%	98.7%	98.1%
Goal	95.0%	95.0%	95.0%	95.0%	95.0%	95.0%	95.0%	95.0%	95.0%	95.0%	95.0%	95.0%	95.0%	95.0%	95.0%

FIGURE 8.4

Schedule adherence.

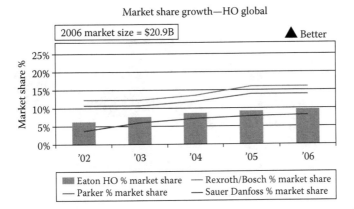

FIGURE 8.5
Market share growth.

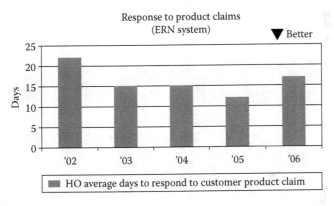

FIGURE 8.6
Response to product claims.

- Figure 8.7: New product market releases
  - The data track new product releases as a measure of innovation.

Financial Results

- Figure 8.8: Revenue trend
  - Organization sales have demonstrated a favorable trend over the five-year period. Acquisitions have accounted for 49% of the total growth, while the remaining 51% has been achieved organically.
- Figure 8.9: Growth by region
  - Sales Compound Annual Growth Rate (CAGR) for the organization is 15% from '02 to '06, which exceeds the corporation's expectations of 10% growth through the cycle. The 15% CAGR

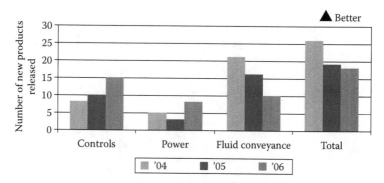

FIGURE 8.7
New product market releases.

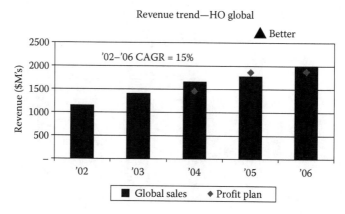

FIGURE 8.8
Revenue trend.

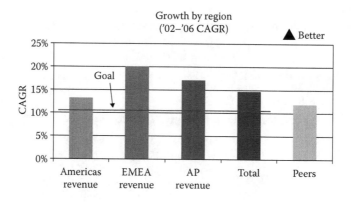

FIGURE 8.9
Compound annual growth rate by region.

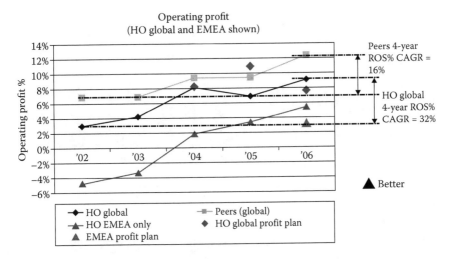

FIGURE 8.10
Operating profit.

has outpaced the growth of the organization peer group, which has grown at 12% CAGR. Peer group companies include Parker Hannifin, Sauer Danfoss, Sun Hydraulics, Oilgear, and Moog Industrial segment.

- Figure 8.10: Operating profit
  - Operating profit margin as a percentage of sales, or Return on Sales (ROS), is shown in Figure 8.10.
  - The organization has made a considerable improvement over this period; thus, the favorable trend is seen.
  - These improvements are attributed to applying focus on cost-out activities, pricing initiatives, manufacturing improvements, and leveraging higher sales volumes.
  - This is especially evident in the profitability improvements in the Europe, Middle East, Africa (EMEA) business.

Human Resource Results

- Figure 8.11: Employee involvement
  - Figure 8.11 shows the Employee Engagement index results from the employee survey.
  - Data show that the organization witnessed an overall 2% decline in this survey dimension, which is attributed to a reduction in

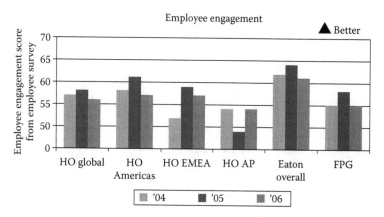

FIGURE 8.11
Employee involvement.

force and Global Manufacturing and Logistic Strategy (GMLS) actions.

- Data results also reveal that facilities more mature in First Line Excellence (FLEX) implementation, on average, scored 5% higher in this survey dimension.
- Figure 8.12: Reduction of lost work days cases (LWDCs) incident rate versus industry week's best plants

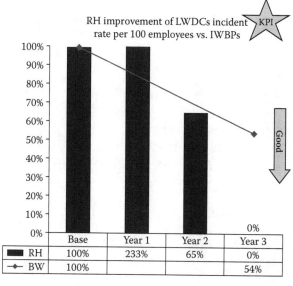

	Base	Year 1	Year 2	Year 3
RH	100%	233%	65%	0%
BW	100%			54%

FIGURE 8.12
Reduction of LWDCs incident rate versus industry week's best plants.

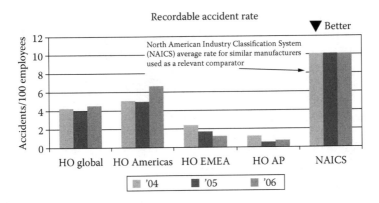

FIGURE 8.13
Safety recordable accident rate.

- Figure 8.13: Safety recordable accident rate
  - The significant reduction in LDWC and accident rates is seen because of
  - Corporate health and safety five-year safety goals
    - 1.0 case total recordable rate
    - 0.2 days away case rate
  - Established short-term goals by work cell or areas
  - Established safety suggestion program
    - Facilitated by employees (safety committee)
    - Recognition for "best" suggestion at monthly plant meetings
  - Job Safety Analysis (JSA) reviews led by employees
- Figure 8.14: Steady improvement in lifelong learning

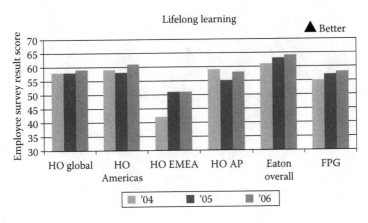

FIGURE 8.14
Steady improvement in lifelong learning.

- Figure 8.14 shows a summary of employee survey responses regarding the dimension of lifelong learning. The bar charts show a steady improvement in this survey dimension as a result of training and development activities.

Organizational Effectiveness Results

- Figure 8.15: First pass yield
  - Definition: Defective parts detected in the final test divided by total parts tested × 1,000,000.
  - 2007 spike is attributed to the recent integration of complex machining operations.
  - Improvement in first pass yield was mainly attributed to the implementation of Global Quality Management System (GQMS), Lean Manufacturing, and Six Sigma.
- Figure 8.16: Cost of nonconformance (CONC)
  - Improvement in CONC was mainly attributed to the implementation of GQMS, Lean Manufacturing, and Six Sigma.
- Figure 8.17: Supplier DPPM
  - Improvement in Supplier DPPM was mainly attributed to the implementation of GQMS, Lean Manufacturing, and Six Sigma.

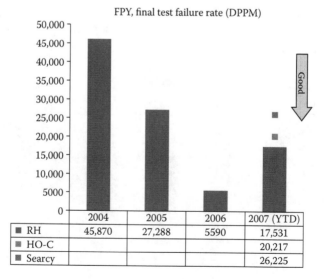

FPY, final test failure rate (DPPM)

	2004	2005	2006	2007 (YTD)
■ RH	45,870	27,288	5590	17,531
■ HO-C				20,217
■ Searcy				26,225

FIGURE 8.15
First pass yield DPPM.

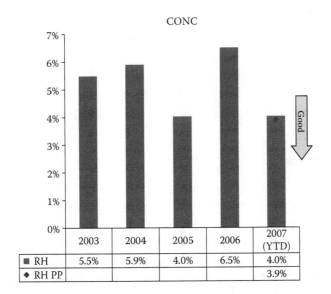

FIGURE 8.16
Cost of nonconformance.

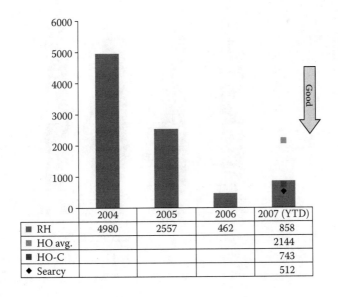

FIGURE 8.17
Supplier DPPM.

- Figure 8.18: Supplier OTD
  - Improvement in Supplier DPPM was mainly attributed to the implementation of GQMS, Lean Manufacturing, and Six Sigma.
- Figure 8.19: Days on hand (DOH) inventory
  - Improvement in Supplier DPPM was mainly attributed to the implementation of GQMS, Lean Manufacturing, and Six Sigma.

Leadership and Social Responsibility Results

- Figure 8.20: Leadership trust survey results
  - Employee Survey Result to a statement: "Leadership Will Take Constructive Action Based on Survey."
  - The result is a proof of the FLEX implementation.
- Figure 8.21: Community development
  - Employee Survey Result on Community Involvement to a statement: "I am encouraged to be active in the community."
  - The result is a proof of the Human Resources (HR) function's excellence.

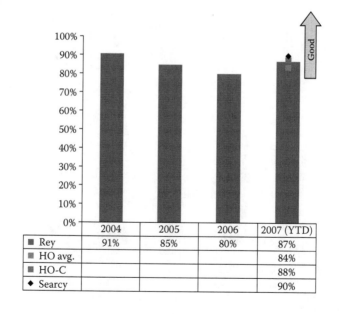

	2004	2005	2006	2007 (YTD)
Rey	91%	85%	80%	87%
HO avg.				84%
HO-C				88%
Searcy				90%

FIGURE 8.18
Supplier OTD.

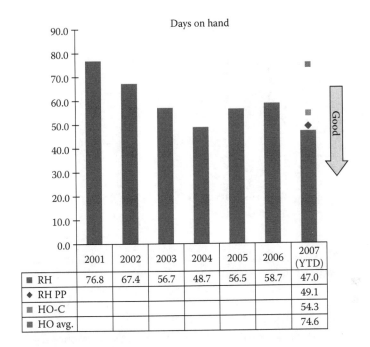

FIGURE 8.19
DOH inventory.

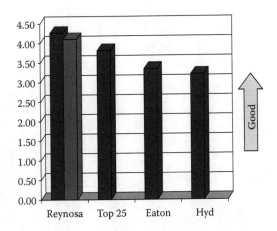

FIGURE 8.20
Leadership trust survey results. Survey Result—Leadership—"Leadership Will Take Constructive Action Based on Survey."

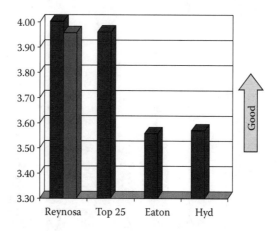

FIGURE 8.21
Community involvement. Annual Survey Result on Community Involvement to a statement: "I am encouraged to be active in the community."

- Figure 8.22: United Way contribution
  - The result is a proof of the HR function's excellence.
- Figure 8.23: Energy consumption
  - The result is a proof of the ISO 14001 implementation.

Product, Service, and Customer-Focused Results

This item examines your organization's key product and service performance results, with the aim of delivering product and service quality that leads to customer satisfaction, loyalty, and positive referral. It also examines your organization's customer-focused performance results, with the

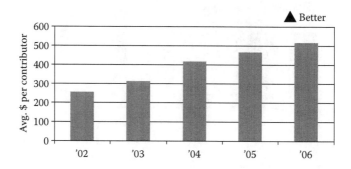

FIGURE 8.22
United Way average employee contribution.

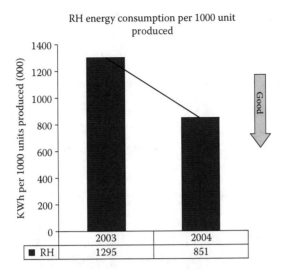

FIGURE 8.23
Energy consumption per 1000 units produced implemented capital projects in cooling towers and capacitor banks to drive improvements in power factor.

aim of demonstrating how well your organization has been satisfying your customers and has developed loyalty, repeat business, and positive referral.

Market Results

Organizations measure and review market results to evaluate performance, identify opportunities for improvement, and determine allocation of resources. This item examines your organization's market results, with the aim of understanding your marketplace challenges and opportunities.

Financial Results

This item examines your organization's financial results, with the aim of understanding your financial sustainability. The trends over a five-year period are recorded to ascertain a planned growth as per the strategic plan is achieved.

Human Resource Results

This item examines your organization's human resource results, with the aim of demonstrating how well your organization has been creating and maintaining a positive, productive, learning, and caring work environment for all employees.

Organizational Effectiveness Results

This item examines your organization's other key operational performance results not reported in the above four items, with the aim of achieving organizational effectiveness and process efficiency.

Leadership and Social Responsibility Results

This item examines your organization's key results in the area of leadership and societal responsibilities, with the aim of maintaining a financially sound, ethical organization that is a good citizen in its communities.

9

Business Excellence Assessment

Time has now come to carry out the self-assessment of the organization's readiness to qualify for the Business Excellence Award. The goal is to deploy the Baldrige criteria as a business model to all of the organization's facilities as a means to drive performance excellence.

The assessment will be based on the LATEST criteria of the BE Model based on Malcolm Baldrige National Quality Award (MBNQA). It is freely available at http://www.nist.gov/baldrige.

Category	Points
1. Leadership	120
2. Strategic Planning	85
3. Customer and Market Focus	85
4. Information and Analysis	90
5. HR Focus	85
6. Process Management	85
7. Business Results	450
Total	1000

ASSESSMENT SCORES FOR CATEGORIES 1 TO 7

Assessment scores are determined as per Baldrige criteria. Categories 1 to 6 are scored as per Figure 9.1.

Assessment score for Results Criteria 7 is scored as per Figure 9.2.

SCORE	DESCRIPTION
0% or 5%	• No SYSTEMATIC APPROACH to item requirements is evident; information is ANECDOTAL. (A) • Little or no DEPLOYMENT of any SYSTEMATIC APPROACH is evident. (D) • An improvement orientation is not evident; improvement is achieved by reacting to problems. (L) • No organizational ALIGNMENT is evident; individual areas or work units operate independently. (I)
10%, 15% 20% or 25%	• The beginning of a SYSTEMATIC APPROACH to the BASIC REQUIREMENTS of the item is evident. (A) • The APPROACH is in the early stages of DEPLOYMENT in most areas or work units, inhibiting progress in achieving the BASIC REQUIREMENTS of the item. (D) • Early stages of a transition from reacting to problems to a general improvement orientation are evident. (L) • The APPROACH is ALIGNED with other areas or work units largely through joint problem solving. (I)
30%, 35% 40% or 45%	• An EFFECTIVE, SYSTEMATIC APPROACH, responsive to the BASIC REQUIREMENTS of the item, is evident. (A) • The APPROACH is DEPLOYED, although some areas or work units are in early stages of DEPLOYMENT. (D) • The beginning of a SYSTEMATIC APPROACH to evaluation and improvement of KEY PROCESSES is evident. (L) • The APPROACH is in the early stages of ALIGNMENT with the basic organizational needs identified in response to the Organizational Profile and other process items. (I)
50%, 55% 60% or 65%	• An EFFECTIVE, SYSTEMATIC APPROACH, responsive to the OVERALL REQUIREMENTS of the item, is evident. (A) • The APPROACH is well DEPLOYED, although DEPLOYMENT may vary in some areas or work units. (D) • A fact-based, SYSTEMATIC evaluation and improvement PROCESS and some organizational LEARNING, including INNOVATION, are in place for improving the efficiency and EFFECTIVENESS of KEY PROCESSES. (L) • The APPROACH is ALIGNED with your overall organizational needs as identified in response to the Organizational Profile and other process items. (I)
70%, 75% 80% or 85%	• An EFFECTIVE, SYSTEMATIC APPROACH, responsive to the MULTIPLE REQUIREMENTS of the item, is evident. (A) • The APPROACH is well DEPLOYED, with no significant gaps. (D) • Fact-based, SYSTEMATIC evaluation and improvement and organizational LEARNING, including INNOVATION, are KEY management tools; there is clear evidence of refinement as a result of organizational-level ANALYSIS and sharing. (L) • The APPROACH is INTEGRATED with your current and future organizational needs as identified in response to the Organizational Profile and other process items. (I)
90%, 95% or 100%	• An EFFECTIVE, SYSTEMATIC APPROACH, fully responsive to the MULTIPLE REQUIREMENTS of the item, is evident. (A) • The APPROACH is fully DEPLOYED without significant weaknesses or gaps in any areas or work units. (D) • Fact-based, SYSTEMATIC evaluation and improvement and organizational LEARNING through INNOVATION are KEY organization-wide tools; refinement and INNOVATION, backed by ANALYSIS and sharing, are evident throughout the organization. (L) • The APPROACH is well INTEGRATED with your current and future organizational needs as identified in response to the Organizational Profile and other process items. (I)

FIGURE 9.1
Scoring guidelines for use with Categories 1 to 6.

GUIDELINES FOR A WELL-WRITTEN COMMENT

A well-written comment addresses the following two guidelines: guidelines for content and guidelines for style, as shown in Figure 9.3.

SCORING SYSTEM

The scoring of responses to criteria items and award applicant feedback are based on two evaluation dimensions: (1) process and (2) results. Criteria users

SCORE	DESCRIPTION
0% or 5%	• There are no organizational PERFORMANCE RESULTS, or the RESULTS reported are poor. (Le) • TREND data either are not reported or show mainly adverse TRENDS. (T) • Comparative information is not reported. (C) • RESULTS are not reported for any areas of importance to the accomplishment of your organization's MISSION. (I)
10%, 15% 20% or 25%	• A few organizational PERFORMANCE RESULTS are reported, responsive to the BASIC REQUIREMENTS of the item, and early good PERFORMANCE LEVELS are evident. (Le) • Some TREND data are reported, with some adverse TRENDS evident. (T) • Little or no comparative information is reported. (C) • RESULTS are reported for a few areas of importance to the accomplishment of your organization's MISSION. (I)
30%, 35% 40% or 45%	• Good organizational PERFORMANCE LEVELS are reported, responsive to the BASIC REQUIREMENTS of the item. (Le) • Some TREND data are reported, and most of the TRENDS presented are beneficial. (T) • Early stages of obtaining comparative information are evident. (C) • RESULTS are reported for many areas of importance to the accomplishment of your organization's MISSION. (I)
50%, 55% 60% or 65%	• Good organizational PERFORMANCE LEVELS are reported, responsive to the OVERALL REQUIREMENTS of the item. (Le) • Beneficial TRENDS are evident in areas of importance to the accomplishment of your organization's MISSION. (T) • Some current PERFORMANCE LEVELS have been evaluated against relevant comparisons and/or BENCHMARKS and show areas of good relative PERFORMANCE. (C) • Organizational PERFORMANCE RESULTS are reported for most KEY student and other CUSTOMER, market, and PROCESS requirements. (I)
70%, 75% 80% or 85%	• Good-to-excellent organizational PERFORMANCE LEVELS are reported, responsive to the MULTIPLE REQUIREMENTS of the item. (Le) • Beneficial TRENDS have been sustained over time in most areas of importance to the accomplishment of your organization's MISSION. (T) • Many to most TRENDS and current PERFORMANCE LEVELS have been evaluated against relevant comparisons and/or BENCHMARKS and show areas of leadership and very good relative PERFORMANCE. (C) • Organizational PERFORMANCE RESULTS are reported for most KEY student and other CUSTOMER, market, PROCESS, and ACTION PLAN requirements. (I)
90%, 95% or 100%	• Excellent organizational PERFORMANCE LEVELS are reported that are fully responsive to the MULTIPLE REQUIREMENTS of the item. (Le) • Beneficial TRENDS have been sustained over time in all areas of importance to the accomplishment of your organization's MISSION. (T) • Industry and BENCHMARK leadership is demonstrated in many areas. (C) • Organizational PERFORMANCE RESULTS and PROJECTIONS are reported for most KEY student and other CUSTOMER, market, PROCESS, and ACTION PLAN requirements. (I)

FIGURE 9.2
Scoring guidelines for use with Category 7.

need to furnish information relating to these dimensions. Specific factors for these dimensions are described below. Scoring guidelines are given in MBNQA Assessment Guidelines.

PROCESS

"Process" refers to the methods your organization uses and improves to address the item requirements in Categories 1–6. The four factors used to evaluate process are Approach, Deployment, Learning, and Integration (A–D–L–I).

Contents Guidelines	Style Guidelines
1. Uses a single, simple, complete thought to clearly specify the strength (using specific examples from the application) or OFI (using specific omissions or problem identified from the application). OFI-Opportunity for Improvement.	1. Uses the applicant's terminology when appropriate.
2. Addresses central requirements of the criteria and does not go beyond the requirements of the Criteria.	2. Uses a polite, professional, and positive tone.
3. Is most relevant and important to the applicant based on its key factors.	3. For Training & Evaluation Week Scorebooks, tell what is missing if something "is not clear." However, do not use "it is not clear" in Award Stage 3 Scorebooks or Certification Feedback Reports.
4. Draws linkages between Items or between an Item and the application's Organizational Profile.	4. Highlights an applicant's substantive strength or OFI, not its writing style or graphics. For example, it avoids phrases such as "should be add remove in Item 3.2," "x axis is not clear," or "is poorly described," because there are criticism of the writing, not the applicant's performance system.
5. Does not contradict other comments found elsewhere in the scorebook. Contradictions may occur when a writer does not clearly specify the strength or opportunity as noted above.	5. Identifies strengths or OFIs according to where the Item falls in the Criteria, not by where the applicant places the information in the applications.
6. Is nonprescriptive. Refrain from using "could," "should," and "would."	6. Uses Vocabulary and phraseology from the Criteria, Core Values, and Scoring Guidelines.
7. Is nonprescriptive. Refrain from using terms such as "good," "bad," or "inadequate." State the observation in a factual manner, e.g., "customer satisfaction rates have increased over the past three years."	7. Avoids jargon and acronyms, unless they are used by the applicant.
	8. In Award Scorebooks provides a figure number when is made to information from a figure.

FIGURE 9.3

Postassessment guidelines for a well-written comment.

"Approach" (A) Refers to

- The methods used to accomplish the process
- The appropriateness of the methods to the item requirements
- The effectiveness of use of the methods
- The degree to which the approach is repeatable and based on reliable data and information (i.e., systematic)

"Deployment" (D) Refers to the Extent to Which

- Your approach is applied in addressing item requirements relevant and important to your organization
- Your approach is applied consistently
- Your approach is used by all appropriate work units

"Learning" (L) Refers to

- Refining your approach through cycles of evaluation and improvement
- Encouraging breakthrough change to your approach through innovation
- Sharing of refinements and innovation with other relevant work units and processes in your organization

"Integration" (I) Refers to the Extent to Which

- Your approach is aligned with your organizational needs identified in other criteria item requirements
- Your measures, information, and improvement systems are complementary across processes and work units
- Your plans, processes, results, analysis, learning, and actions are harmonized

---

RESULTS

"Results" refers to your organization's outputs and outcomes in achieving the requirements in Chapter 8. The factors used to evaluate results are as follows:

Performance Levels (Le)

- Your current level of performance

Trends (T)

- Rate (i.e., slope of trend data) and breadth (i.e., how widely deployed and shared) of your performance improvements

Comparisons (C)

- Your performance relative to appropriate comparisons and benchmarks

Linkages (Li)

- Linkage of your results measures (often through segmentation) to important customer, product and service, market, process, and action plan performance requirements identified in your organizational profile and in process items

Gaps (G)

- The absence of a result that is required to be reported in a particular item is absent

The Certification Plan for all units of the organization

- Every applicable business unit is required to be certified.
- Any business unit that is certified and earns a score of 500 points or more will be reassessed in three years. Those certified with scores of less than 500 points will be reassessed in two years.
- The schedule for all plant assessments will be set according to the schedule for their business regardless of their score.
- All newly acquired facilities must have a BE baseline assessment completed 12 months after closing.

Continual improvement in the scores required translates into progress in the organizational performance. Table 9.1 suggests a plan for the first three years for a typical plant to achieve a score of 500 points.

TABLE 9.1

Suggested Three Year Scoring Plan for BE Certification Process

Plant Certification—BEA Scores Required			
Certification Cycle	Overall Scores	Category Scores	Effective Date
First assessment	400	40%	3/11
Second assessment	450	40%	6/12
Third assessment	500	40%	6/13

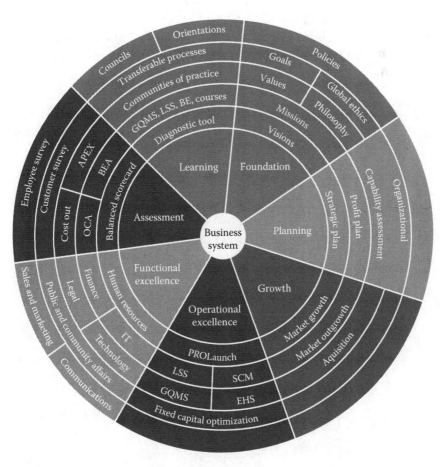

FIGURE 9.4

Circular chart: Business Excellence System Framework.

CIRCULAR CHART FOR EXCELLENT BUSINESS SYSTEM FRAMEWORK

The assessment touches each and every field described in the following circular chart for Excellent Business System Framework.

The circular chart shown in Figure 9.4 is an excellent guide summarizing the entire Business Excellence System Framework. In these four related books, I have endeavored to describe all elements in a simple and easy-to-understand manner. By following the book *Business Excellence: Exceeding Your Customers' Expectations Each Time, All the Time*, it will be possible to attain a score of at least 400/1000 points in the first year, and as the years go by in the pursuit of excellence and proactively taking actions on all OFIs (opportunities for improvement) after each assessment, the organization can become one of the top admired businesses of the world.

Conclusion

Business Excellence Models can lead an organization on a path of excellence, but it is really up to the leadership team to get their act together and make the organization a top world-class sustainable institution.

Today's global competition and information technology have created the "Improvement Imperative." There is an urgent need to improve around the globe to remain competitive.

All measures of performance like Quality (Q), Cost (C), and Delivery (D) are affected by all parts of the business. A single improvement focus is helpful but is not enough.

Reducing waste and cycle time through Lean implementation is necessary but not sufficient. Reducing variation through Six Sigma application alone will not make you a winner.

An all-pervading view of facing global competition is to adopt a Business Excellence (BE) strategy. BE is a process

- That works in all areas of the business
- That works in all cultures—common language and tool set
- That can address all measures of performance
- That addresses all aspects of process management: process design, improvement, and control
- That can address all types of improvement: flow, variation, optimization, robustness, and so on
- Where management process for improvement exists: plans, goals, budgets, and reviews
- That focuses on developing an improvement culture
- That uses improvement as a leadership development tool

Comprehensive Improvement Management Reviews as summarized in the following table are a key to BE strategy.

Review Team	Review Timing
Process operators	Daily
Process managers and staff	Weekly
Site manager and staff	Monthly
Business manager and staff	Quarterly

Bibliography

AIAG 2001 PFMEA 3rd edition.

AIAG 2001 MSA 3rd edition.

AIAG 2005 SPC 3rd edition.
>   American Society for Quality ASQ's
>   Foundations in Quality Learning Series
>   Certified Manager of Quality/Organizational Excellence
>   Certified Quality Auditor
>   Certified Quality Engineer

Argyris, C. and D. A. Schon (1978) *Organizational Learning: A Theory of Action Perspective.* ISBN-13: 978-0201001747.

Crosby, P. (2005) "Crosby's 14 Steps to Improvement," *Quality Progress*, 60–64.

Crosby, P. (1984) *Quality without Tears.* New York: McGraw-Hill.

Deming, W. E. (1993) *The New Economics for Industry, Government, Education.* 2nd ed. Cambridge, MA: MIT Press.

Deming, E. (1986) *Out of the Crisis.* Cambridge, MA: MIT Press.

Gryna, F. M., R. C. H. Chua, and J. A. DeFeo (2005) *Juran's Quality Planning and Analysis for Enterprise Quality.* 5th ed. New York: McGraw-Hill.

Hoer, R. W. and R. D. Sneer (2010) "Continuous Improvement Systems—The Next Big Thing beyond Lean Six Sigma," *Six Sigma Forum Magazine.*

Masaaki, I. (1997) *Gemba Kaizen*, New York: McGraw-Hill.

MBQNA Business Excellence Criteria.

Pyzdek, T. (2003) *The Six Sigma Handbook: A Complete Guide for Green Belts, Black Belts, and Managers at All Levels*, 2nd ed. New York: McGraw-Hill.

Shigeo, S. (2005) A study of the Toyota Production System by Andrew Dillon.

Sneer, R. D. (2008) "What Improvement System Should Your Organization Use—A Commentary on the Shining System?," *Quality Engineering*, Volume 20, No. 1, 23–26.

Sneer, R. D. and E. C. Gardner (2008) "Putting It All Together—Continuous Improvement is Better than Postponed Perfection," *Quality Progress*, October 2008, 56–59.

The Toyota Production System, www.toyota Georgetown.com/tps.asp.

Visual-Lean Institute (Gwendolyn Galsworth 1997).

Wheeler, D. J. (1995) *Advanced Topics in Statistical Process Control.* Knoxville, TN: SPC Press.

Womack, J. P. (2011) *Gemba Walks*, Lean Enterprise Institute.

Glossary

5S: Stands for five Japanese words that begin with the letter "S." The words as translated in English are as follows: Seiri = Sort, Seiton = Straighten or Set in order, Seso = Shine, Seiketsu = Standardize, and Shitsuke = Sustain. Altogether, they mean orderly, well-organized, well-inspected, clean, and efficient workplaces.

5 Whys: A simple process of determining the root cause of a problem by asking "why" after each situation to drive deeper in more detail to arrive at the root cause of an issue.

7 Wastes: Originally identified by Taiichi Ohno, these are as follows: (1) overproduction, (2) waiting, (3) transportation, (4) overprocessing, (5) stock on hand, (6) movement, and (7) making defective product.

8D: This is a popular method for problem solving because it is reasonably easy to teach and effective. The 8D steps and tools used are as follows:

D0: Prepare for the 8D
D1: Form a team
D2: Describe the problem
D3: Interim containment action
D4: RCA (root cause analysis) and escape point
D5: Permanent corrective action
D6: Implement and validate
D7: Prevention
D8: Closure and team celebration

This process is known as Global 8D by Ford.

A3: It is a report prepared on an 11″ × 17″ plain paper by the owner of the issue. The PDCA format is used. It gathers current information and analysis, creates goals and metrics, and builds buy-in from stakeholders.

Anon: Japanese word meaning light or lantern. It is a form of communication for abnormal condition or machine malfunction. It often resembles a stop traffic light where red = stop, yellow = caution, and green = go. Another form can be an Andon cord, which is pulled by the operator to communicate abnormal situation.

APEX: Achieving Performance Excellence.

AS 9100: It is a widely adopted and standardized quality management system for the aerospace industry.

BE: Business Excellence.

BEA: Business Excellence Assessment.

Black Belt: A professional who can explain and practice Six Sigma philosophies and principles, including supporting systems and tools.

BMT: Business Management Team.

BPR: Business process reengineering (BPR) is the analysis and redesign of workflow within and between enterprises. BPR reached its maximum popularity in the early 1990s.

BS: Business System.

Budget: An estimate of costs, revenues, and resources over a specified period, reflecting a reading of future financial conditions and goals.

CA: Corrective action taken to eliminate the cause of the nonconformity.

Cause-and-Effect Diagram: This diagram-based technique helps us identify all of the likely causes of the problems faced in working environments.

Changeover: Setting up a machine or production line to make a different part, number, or product.

Changeover Time: The time from the last good piece of the current production run to the first good piece of the next run.

CONC: Cost of nonconformance: scrap, warranty, premium freight, overtime, rework divided by sales.

Constraint: Anything that limits a system from achieving higher performance. It is also called a bottleneck.

Continual Improvement: Continual indicates duration of improvement that continues over a long period, but with intervals of interruption. For example, the plant modification disrupted by logistics/traffic for nearly two years.

Continuous Improvement: An approach of making frequent and small changes to process whose cumulative results lead to higher levels of quality, cost, and efficiency.

Countermeasure: Corrective action taken to address problems or abnormalities.

CRR: Customer Relationship Review.

Customer: A party that receives or consumes products (goods or services) and who has the ability to choose between different products.

Cycle: A sequence of operations repeated regularly.

Cycle Time: The time for one sequence of operations to occur.

DOH: Days on Hand inventory.

DPMO: Defect per Million Opportunities.

DPO: Days Payables Outstanding.

Effectiveness: The degree to which objectives are achieved and the extent to which targeted problems are solved. In contrast to efficiency, effectiveness is determined without reference to costs and, whereas efficiency means "doing the thing right," effectiveness means "doing the right thing."

EFQM: European Foundation for Quality Management.

EHS: Environmental Health and Safety.

Equipment Availability: The percentage of time equipment (or process) is available to run. This is sometimes called "uptime."

ERP: Enterprise Resource Planning.

Error Proofing: See Poka-Yoke.

External Setup: Procedures that can be performed while a machine is running.

FAI: First article inspection.

FIFO: "First-in, First-out"; in other words, material produced by one process is consumed in the same order (FIFO) by the next process.

Fishbone Diagram: The fishbone diagram identifies many possible causes for an effect or problem. It can be used to structure a brainstorming session. It immediately sorts ideas into useful categories. Major categories of causes of the problem are as follows:

> Methods
> Machines (equipment)
> People (manpower)
> Materials
> Measurement
> Environment

Flow: The completion of steps within a value stream so that product or service "flows" from the beginning of the value stream to the customer without waste.

Flow Production: Same as Flow.

FMEA: Failure Mode and Effects Analysis (FMEA) is a step-by-step approach for identifying all possible failures in a design, a manufacturing or assembly process, or a product or service. "Failure modes" means the ways, or modes, in which something might fail. Failures are any errors or defects, especially ones that affect the customer, and can be potential or actual. "Effects analysis" refers to studying the consequences of those failures.

FPY: First pass yield. It is defined as the number of units coming out of a process divided by the number of units going into that process over a specified period. Only good units with no rework are counted as coming out of an individual process. Also known as TPY—throughput yield.

Gemba: Japanese word meaning "real place," where action takes place—a shop floor or work areas.

Gemba Walk: A walk carried out by a coach (a lean Sensei) and student or students to look for abnormal conditions, waste, or opportunities for improvement.

GQMS: Global Quality Management System.

Heijunka: A method for leveling production for mix and volume.

Hoshin Kanri: A strategic decision-making tool used for policy deployment.

Internal Setup: Procedures that must be performed while the machine is stopped.

Ishikawa Diagram: See Fishbone Diagram.

Jidoka: A device that stops production or equipment when a defective condition arises. Attention is drawn to this condition and the operator who stopped the production. Jidoka system has faith in the operator who is trained in the job.

Just in Time (JIT): Originally developed by TPS (Toyota Production System). JIT presupposes that all waste is eliminated from the production line and only the inventory in the right quantity and at the right time is used for the production where the rate of production is exactly as required by the customer.

Kaikaku: Japanese word meaning innovation or a radical breakthrough. Kaikaku requires radical thinking and takes more time in planning and implementation.

Kaizen: Japanese word meaning change for the better or do good. It is a process of making continual improvements by everyone keeping in mind the quality and safety.

Kaizen Event: A short team-based improvement project. Also called Kaizen Blitz.

Kanban: Means "sign board" or a label. It serves as an instruction for production and replenishment.

KBD: Key Business Driver.

KBF: Key Business Factor.

KCC: Key Critical Characteristic.

KPC: Key Performance Characteristic.

KPI: Key Performance Indicator.

KSM: Key Support Measure.

Lead Time: A time required to move one piece from the time order is taken until it is shipped to the customer.

Line Balancing: It is a technique where all operations are evenly balanced and staffing is also balanced to meet the takt time.

LSS: Lean Six Sigma.

Manufacturing Resource Planning (MRP II): Unlike MRP it takes into consideration the capacity planning and finance requirement. It works out alternative production plans through the simulation tool.

Materials Requirement Planning (MRP): It is a computerized system of determining quantity and timing requirements for production and delivery of products for customers as well as suppliers. This is a PUSH production system.

MBNQA: Stands for Malcolm Baldrige National Quality Award. It is an award given to the organization for achieving the highest quality standard.

MESH: Management of Environment, Safety, and Health.

Milk Run: The routing of supply and delivery trucks/vehicles to make multiple pickups and deliveries at various locations to reduce transportation waste.

MPS: Market Product Specification.

Muda: Japanese word for waste. It is an element that does not add value to the product or service. Also known as no-value-added activity carried out on a product or service that does not add value and the customer will not pay for it.

Mura: Japanese word for variability or unevenness.

Muri: Japanese word for physical and mental strain or overburden.

One (Single) Piece Flow: Practiced in JIT system where one work piece flows from process to process to minimize waste.

Operational Excellence (OpEx): An element of organizational initiative that stresses the application of a variety of principles, systems, and tools toward the sustainable improvement of key performance metrics. This philosophy is based on continuous improvement, such as Quality Management System, Lean Manufacturing, and

Six Sigma. Operational Excellence goes beyond the traditional methods of improvement and leads to a long-term change in organizational culture.

OTD: On-time delivery.

Overall Equipment Effectiveness (OEE): It is a product of the following key measures:

1. Operational availability
2. Performance efficiency
3. First pass yield quality

PAIP: A process for performance analysis and improvement.

Paynter Chart: A graphical tool started at Ford Motor Company that combines the concepts of a run chart with a Pareto chart.

PCP: Process control plan.

PDA: Personal Digital Assistant.

PDCA: Plan–do–check–act cycle for continual improvement.

PFMEA: Process Failure Mode and Effects Analysis.

Point-of-use storage (POUS): Storing or keeping materials, tools, information, and items near to where they are used.

Poka-Yoke: Also known as Mistake Proofing. "Poka" in Japanese means inadvertent mistake and "Yoke" means prevention. These can be simple, low-cost devices to sophisticated electromechanical devices to prevent production of defective product.

Process: Sequence of interdependent and linked procedures that, at every stage, consume one or more resources (employee time, energy, machines, money) to convert inputs (data, material, parts, etc.) into outputs. These outputs then serve as inputs for the next stage until a known goal or end result is reached.

Product Realization: The term used to describe the work that the organization goes through to develop, manufacture, and deliver the finished product or service to the customer.

Productivity: It is measured as an output for a given input. Productivity increase is critical to improving living standards.

Pull: Alternatively known as pull production where the upstream supplier does not produce until the downstream customer signals the need.

Push: Alternatively known as push production where the upstream supplier produces as much as it can without regard to the fact whether the downstream customer needs it or not.

PWP: Personnel Work Policy.

QOS: Quality Operating System originally implemented by Ford. The methodology was established to measure the effectiveness of the quality system and to drive continuous improvement.

RPN: Stands for Risk Priority Number. In FMEA, RPN = Severity × Occurrence × Detection.

RTY: Rolled throughput yield. It is a probability that a single piece will pass through all production steps without a single defect.

SCM: Supply Chain Management.

Shadow Board: A board where each tool has a place; it helps determine which tools are missing.

Single Minute Exchange of Dies (SMED): A group of techniques developed by Shiego Shingo for changeover of production equipment in less than ten minutes.

SIOP: Sales, Inventory, and Operation Planning. A holistic process that will help SCM keep demand and supply balanced.

SIPOC: A process identification where the requirements for Supplier, Input, Process steps, Output, and Customer are defined.

Six Sigma: A set of tools and techniques for process improvement. It is originally developed by Motorola in 1981.

SOX: The *Sarbanes–Oxley* Act of 2002 (often shortened to SOX) is legislation passed by the U.S. Congress to protect shareholders and the general public from accounting errors and fraudulent practices in the enterprise, as well as improve the accuracy of corporate disclosures.

Spaghetti Diagram: A diagram showing layout and flow of information, material and people in a work area. It is generally used to highlight motion and transportation waste.

SPC: Statistical Process Controls for quality control where process variations are measured and controlled.

Standard Work: An accurate description of every process step specifying takt time, cycle time, and minimum inventory needed and sequence of each process step. The entire process is carried out with minimum human motion and other wastes.

Super Market: Part storage before they go to the next operation. The parts are managed using minimum and maximum inventory levels.

Sustainability: Continued development or growth, without significant deterioration of the environment and depletion of natural resources on which human well-being depends.

SWOT: It stands for Strength, Weakness, Opportunity, and Threat. Strength and Weakness analysis guides us to identify the positives and negatives inside your organization (S–W) while Opportunity and Threat analysis guides us to identify positives and negatives outside of it. Developing a full SWOT analysis can help with strategic planning and decision making.

System: ASQ (American Society for Quality) defines system as "a group of interdependent processes and people that together perform a common mission."

Takt Time: Available production time divided by the rate of the customer demand.

TPM: Total Productive Maintenance is a system to ensure that every production process machine is able to perform its required tasks such that production is not interrupted.

TQM: Total Quality Management is a management approach that originated in the 1950s. The TQM culture requires quality in all aspects of the company's operations, with processes being done right the first time and defects and waste eradicated from operations.

To be successful in implementing TQM, an organization must concentrate on the following eight key elements:

1. Ethics
2. Integrity
3. Trust
4. Training
5. Teamwork
6. Leadership
7. Recognition
8. Communication

VAA: Value-Added Activity.

VA/VE: Value Analysis/Value Engineering.

Value: It is a capability provided to a customer at the right time at an appropriate price and is defined by the customer.

Value Stream: Sequence of actions required to design, produce, and provide a specific good or service, and along which information, materials, and worth flows.

VOC: Voice of the Customer.

VP: Vice President.

VSM: Value Stream Mapping.

Index

Page numbers ending in "f" refer to figures. Page numbers ending in "t" refer to tables.

About the Author

Suresh Patel is a former Technical Director and Operations Excellence Executive. He holds a BE degree in electrical engineering from M.S. University of Baroda, India, a Master's degree in production technology from South Bank University, London, and an MBA degree from the University of Texas at Brownsville. He is qualified as a Certified Reliability Engineer, Certified Quality Engineer, and Certified Management Systems Auditor by the American Society for Quality.

In his long career spanning more than four decades, he has developed a wide range of products/processes and has helped in establishing six manufacturing plants in India and five U.S. plants in Mexico. Starting with India, his career path has enabled him to work in industries in the UK, Denmark, Belgium, Canada, U.S., China, Mexico, and Chile. His career has been enriched through holding key positions with such multinational corporations as Gestetner, Motorola, United Lighting Technologies, Eaton Corporation, and Fiat Global.

Mr. Patel's practical expertise and interests include establishing Business Excellence Strategies starting from product quality strategies, quality improvement tools deployment, and execution, leading to improvements in product/process delivery performance and reduction in product escapes and product/process variation through Lean Six Sigma and overall business excellence employing Leadership and Results "Triades" as defined in MBNQA USA. Mr. Patel's other interests include supply chain management, manufacturing management, and building technological capabilities in manufacturing firms.